O9-AIF-619

İSTANBUL
ENCOUNTER

VIRGINIA MAXWELL

İstanbul Encounter

Published by Lonely Planet Publications Pty Ltd
ABN 36 005 607 983

Australia	Head Office, Locked Bag 1, Footscray, Victoria 3011 ☎ 03 8379 8000 fax 03 8379 8111 talk2us@lonelyplanet.com.au
USA	150 Linden St, Oakland, CA 94607 ☎ 510 250 6400 toll free 800 275 8555 fax 510 893 8572 info@lonelyplanet.com
UK	2nd fl, 186 City Rd, London EC1V 2NT ☎ 020 7106 2100 fax 020 7106 2101 go@lonelyplanet.co.uk

This title was commissioned in Lonely Planet's London office and produced by: **Commissioning Editor** Clifton Wilkinson **Coordinating Editor** Jeanette Wall **Coordinating Cartographer** Andy Rojas **Layout Designer** Carlos Solarte **Assisting Editor** Alison Ridgway **Managing Editors** Imogen Bannister, Brigitte Ellemor **Managing Cartographers** Alison Lyall, Herman So **Managing Layout Designers** Indra Kilfoyle, Celia Wood **Cover Research** Naomi Parker **Internal Image Research** Aude Vauconsant **Thanks to** Frank Deim, Lisa Knights, Trent Paton, Lyahna Spencer

Printed by Toppan Security Printing Pte. Ltd.
Printed in Singapore

Lonely Planet and the Lonely Planet logo are trademarks of Lonely Planet and are registered in the US Patent and Trademark Office and in other countries.

MIX
Paper from
responsible sources
FSC™ C021741
FSC
www.fsc.org

HOW TO USE THIS BOOK
Colour-Coding & Maps
Colour-coding is used for symbols on maps and in the text that they relate to (eg all eating venues on the maps and in the text are given a green knife and fork symbol). Each neighbourhood also gets its own colour, and this is used down the edge of the page and throughout that neighbourhood section.

Send us your feedback We love to hear from travellers – your comments keep us on our toes and help make our books better. Our well-travelled team reads every word on what you loved or loathed about this book. Although we cannot reply individually to postal submissions, we always guarantee that your feedback goes straight to the appropriate authors, in time for the next edition. Each person who sends us information is thanked in the next edition, and the most useful submissions are rewarded with a free book.
Visit **lonelyplanet.com** to submit your updates and suggestions or to ask for help. Our award-winning website also features inspirational travel stories, news and discussions.
Note: We may edit, reproduce and incorporate your comments in Lonely Planet products such as guidebooks, websites and digital products, so let us know if you don't want your comments reproduced or your name acknowledged. For a copy of our privacy policy visit **lonelyplanet.com/privacy**.

VIRGINIA MAXWELL

After working for many years as a publishing
manager at Lonely Planet's Melbourne head-
quarters, Virginia decided that she'd be happier
writing guidebooks rather than commissioning
them. Since making this decision she's authored
Lonely Planet books to Turkey, Egypt, Spain, Italy,
Lebanon, Morocco, Syria and the United Arab
Emirates. Virginia knows İstanbul well, and loves
it to bits. She is the author of Lonely Planet's
İstanbul City Guide and also writes about the city
for a host of international newspapers and magazines. She usually travels with partner Peter and
young son Max, who have grown to love the city as much as she does.

VIRGINIA'S THANKS

Many thanks to Peter, Max, Pat Yale, René Ames, Tahir Karabaş, Eveline
Zoutendijk, Saffet Tonguç, Barbara Nadel, Ercan and Şenay Tanrıvermiş,
Ann and Tina Nevans, Jennifer Gaudet, Özlem Tuna, Shellie Corman,
Mehmet Umur, Emel Güntaş, Faruk Boyacı, Özen Dalgın, Selin Rozanes,
Necdet and Ayse Bezmen, Atilla Tuna, Verity Campbell and the many lo-
cals who shared their knowledge and love of the city with me. At Lonely
Planet, many thanks to Cliff Wilkinson for giving me the gig.

Our Readers Many thanks to the travellers who wrote to us with helpful hints, useful advice and interesting anecdotes:
Hilde Bennenbroek, Imran Mohammed, Rosa Smith, Maarten van Reeden

Cover photograph Blue tiles at Topkapı Palace, by Sinan Cakmak/Images and Stories. **Internal photographs** p91 Helen
Cathcart/Alamy; p17 sculpture by Ilhan Koman/photo by Rebecca Erol/Alamy; p22 Ali Kabas/Alamy; p76 Alp Korfalı; p20
Yoray Liberman/Getty Images; p30 Roy Mathers/Alamy; p61 Serhat Özşen; p136 Mustafa Ozer/Getty Images; p85 David
Pearson/Alamy; p88 Yucel Tunca p24 Didar Yesilyurt/Istanbul Foundation for Culture and Arts. All other photographs by
Lonely Planet Images, and by Olivier Cirendini p16; Christina Dameyer p4; John Elk III p6; Greg Elms p6, p14, p69, p131,
p132, p133; Jeff Greenberg p137; Tim Hughes p124; Corinne Humphrey p130; Izzet Keribar p12, p19, p25, p26, p111, p115,
p129, p135; Jean-Pierre Lescourret p15, p38; Diego Lezama p18; Diana Mayfield p117; Adina Tovy Amsel p28, p128; Phil
Weymouth p6, p8, p11, p13, p25, p26, p36, p41, p47, p56, p64, p74, p80, p97, p104, p107, p121, p122, p138, p139.

All images are copyright of the photographers unless otherwise indicated. Many of the images in this guide are available for
licensing from **Lonely Planet Images:** www.lonelyplanetimages.com.

A girl finds an appreciative pigeon audience on the steps of the New Mosque (p53)

CONTENTS

THIS IS İSTANBUL

Ask any local to describe what they love about their hometown and they'll shrug, give a small smile and say merely that there is no other place like it. And guess what? They're absolutely right.

There are plenty of cities as big and as full of life as İstanbul, but few where the energy literally seems to crackle in the air. Here, a population conservatively estimated to number 14 million goes about its day-to-day activities with purpose and panache, inspired by the prospect of a bright, EU-flavoured future. That said, locals aren't steered by visions of the future alone. Though it has always been greater than the sum of its monuments, İstanbul is a city where the memory of past glories – and there are lots of them – still shapes the collective consciousness and fuels its aspirations.

Neighbourhoods throughout the city are home to magnificent monuments and structures built in Byzantine or Ottoman times, many of which were given the expert restorations they so richly deserved when İstanbul was a European Capital of Culture in 2010. For the visitor keen to explore on foot, these historical layers of the city are quick to reveal themselves, accompanied by an evocative soundtrack of muezzins duelling from the tops of their minarets and ferries honking their bass-tones horns while crossing between Europe and Asia.

The character of the contemporary city is also multilayered. On your walk, you may pass a traditional Turkish *meyhane* (tavern) packed with boisterous family groups, a sleek rooftop bar/restaurant serving up Noma-inspired dishes to young professionals, a *çay bahçesi* (tea garden) full of nargileh-puffing Anatolian gents, or an outlet of a multinational coffee chain dispensing mocha lattes to a clientele of headscarf-adorned women. They and the other locals you will encounter are bound to make you feel welcome – and lead you to agree that this city truly is like no other.

Top left The New Mosque (p53) looms over Galata Bridge (p52), a picturesque spot for angling **Top right** A meeting of opposites: an old-fashioned tram runs along modern, bustling İstiklal Caddesi (p16) **Bottom** Dervishes (p75) whirling for enlightenment

>HIGHLIGHTS

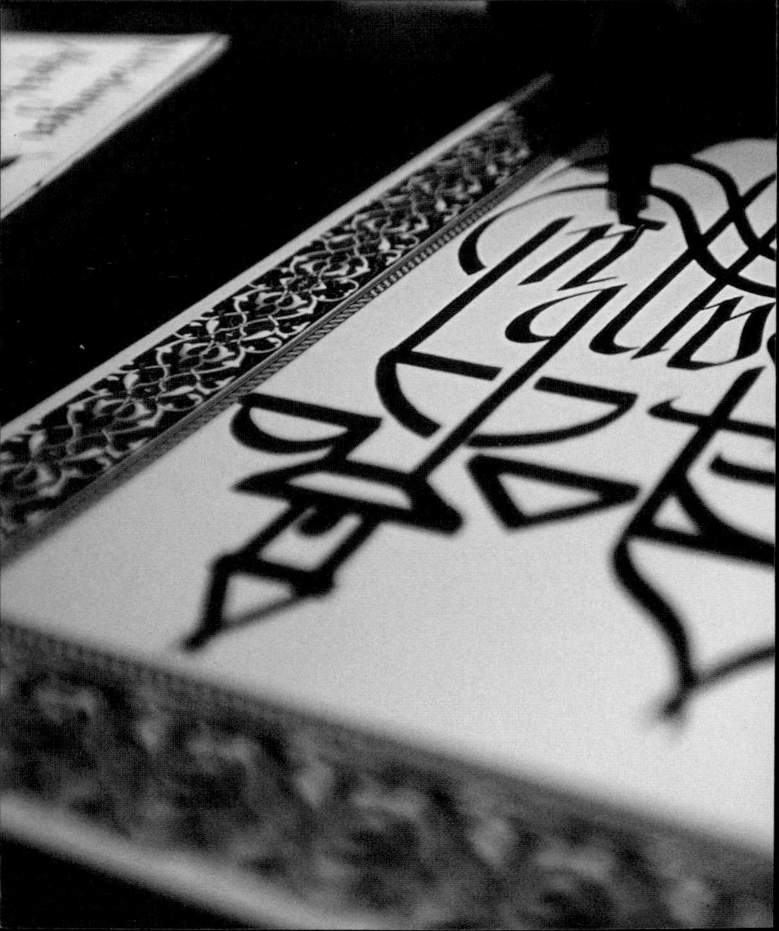

A calligrapher practices his art at the Grand Bazaar (Kapalı Çarşı; p52)

>1 TOPKAPI PALACE

UNCOVER THE SORDID SECRETS OF THE SERAGLIO AT TOPKAPI PALACE

Opulent Topkapı Palace (Topkapı Sarayı) is the subject of more colourful stories than most of the world's royal residences put together. It was home to Selim the Sot, who drowned after drinking too much champagne; İbrahim the Mad, who lost his reason after being imprisoned for 22 years by his brother Murat IV; and the malevolent Roxelana, a former concubine who became the powerful consort of Süleyman the Magnificent.

These three are only a few of the mad, sad and downright bad Ottomans who lived here between 1465 and 1830. Extravagant relics of their centuries of folly, intrigue, excess and war are everywhere you look. You'll see extensive manicured gardens that were once lit by candles riding on tortoises' backs, exquisite tile-encrusted pavilions where royal circumcisions were performed, and golden viewing platforms where the sultans looked upon the Golden Horn (Haliç) and perhaps regretted their sequestered lifestyles. Here great victories in battle were celebrated with lavish banquets presided over by the sultan. Contemporary accounts written by overawed foreign dignitaries marvelled at the palace's legendary staff of black eunuchs, its famed musicians and its elegant purpose-built pavilions.

The palace collections are no less impressive. Started by Mehmet the Conqueror, they were expanded by a succession of sultans who were as interested in philosophy and the arts as they were in conquest and concubines. Sparkling jewels from every corner of the empire are kept in the Treasury, lavish costumes are on display in the Dormitory of the Expeditionary Force, important Islamic relics are housed in the Sacred Safekeeping Rooms and other treasures can be admired in the temporary exhibition spaces next to the Sacred Safekeeping Rooms and in the Imperial Stables.

Walking through the architecturally magnificent Harem, it's easy to forget that women spent their entire lives here under lock and key. That's if they lived for long at all – legend has it that İbrahim the Mad had his entire harem of 280 women tied in sacks and thrown into the Bosphorus when he tired of them.

Allow at least half a day to properly view the palace. Don't miss the Harem or the Treasury, which is home to the jewel-encrusted dagger that's the object of desire in the 1964 film *Topkapi*. And make sure that you walk all the way to the fourth court, with its richly decorated buildings surrounding a serenely beautiful reflective pool.

See p39 for more information.

>2 AYA SOFYA

MARVEL AT ONE OF THE WORLD'S TRULY GREAT BUILDINGS: AYA SOFYA

İstanbul has many architectural masterpieces, but one building surpasses the rest due to its innovative form, historical importance and sheer beauty. Venerable Aya Sofya – built by the great Byzantine emperor Justinian and coveted by the Ottomans for centuries before Mehmet the Conqueror finally stormed into the city to claim it for Islam – has all of this and more, making it an essential stop on every itinerary.

The somewhat squat exterior doesn't promise much, but wait till you see the mesmerising interior! Words can't do it justice; this space truly makes the soul soar and the senses sharpen. As you enter via the imperial door, your gaze is drawn irresistibly to the massive dome, which seems to hover unsupported. Numerous glass windows endow the space with a magical half-light enhanced by the glint of golden mosaics covering the dome and hiding in shadowy corners. It is simply sublime.

History resonates here. The interior is still predominantly Byzantine in form and decoration, but there's an Ottoman overlay of chandeliers, ablution basins and medallions inscribed with fine Arabic calligraphy. Close your eyes and imagine Byzantines celebrating the liturgy, Crusaders storming the main door, Muslims bowing their heads to Allah and the staunchly secular Atatürk striding in to declare it a museum in 1935.

See p36 for more information.

>3 ROOFTOP VIEWS

COMBAT VERTIGO AND ADMIRE THE WORLD'S MOST STUPENDOUS SKYLINE

Most great cities have a signature skyline view that graces a million postcards – İstanbul has enough of them to fill an entire album. The seven hills of the Old City are crowned with a collection of imperial mosques that offer a visual wham-bam unlike any other. With their delicate minarets, distinctive domes and curvaceous outer casings, they dominate the peninsula's skyline and provide romantic backdrops for diners at terrace restaurants around Eminönü and Beyoğlu. See p63 and p80 for places where an Old City view accompanies the menu.

Around Sultanahmet, a Blue Mosque (Sultan Ahmet Camii) or Sea of Marmara view is the main selling point for the battalion of hotels vying for the tourist dollar. And fair enough, too, as there's something quite wonderful about breakfasting on a terrace while looking upon such beauty. See p127 for our guide to the best rooftop terraces in town.

Cross the Galata Bridge (Galata Köprüsü) and the views are deliciously different. Here you can drink among the stars – the real things, not C-list celebs. Rooftops high across the Beyoğlu skyline are home to bars and restaurants with breathtaking views of the Old City, across to Asia and down the Bosphorus. Settle in at one of these for a sunset drink and you will have signed, sealed and delivered your number-one holiday highlight. See p131 for a rundown of our favourite rooftop bars.

>4 BAZAAR DISTRICT

JOIN THE CRUSH AND LOSE YOURSELF IN THE ATMOSPHERIC BAZAAR DISTRICT

The bazaar district – stretching from the Grand Bazaar (Kapalı Çarşı) down to Eminönü on the Golden Horn – is chaotic and colourful. While glam İstinye Park (p100) may be ground zero for sophisticated shoppers on the other side of the Golden Horn, serious *bayanlar* (ladies) bring their sharpened elbows here. Stroll through the hidden Ottoman *hans* (caravanserais) and labyrinthine shopping streets, where the waft of cinnamon and clove intensifies as you approach the historic Spice Bazaar (Mısır Çarşısı, pictured above). You'll see handcarts full of ripe strawberries and green plums, stores displaying sculptural pyramids of spices and olives, and shops selling everything from gaudy circumcision robes to sensible *pardesüler* (gabardines worn by devout Muslim women).

Kick off at the Grand Bazaar and then exit through the Mahmutpaşa Gate (Mahmutpaşa Kapısı), following busy Mahmutpaşa Yokuşu downhill to the Spice Bazaar and its jumble of produce stalls. Here, you can stock up on Turkish delight, buy copper coffee pots, snack on freshly roasted nuts and pop into the delightful tile-encrusted Rüstem Paşa Mosque to enjoy a momentary respite from the crowds.

Allow at least half a day (Monday to Saturday only) for your visit, but be warned – you could spend a month exploring and still only uncover a fraction of this district's delights. See p50 for more information.

>5 FERRY TRIPS

CLIMB ABOARD İSTANBUL'S FAMOUS FLOTILLA OF FERRIES

In the 18th and 19th centuries, the Bosphorus and Golden Horn were alive with caïques (long, thin rowboats), their oars dipping rhythmically into the currents as they carried the sultan and his courtiers from palace to pavilion, and from Europe to Asia. The caïques are long gone, but in their place are the sleek speedboats of the moneyed elite and the much-loved public ferries used by the rest of İstanbul's population.

Spanned by two mammoth bridges, and with a third on the drawing board, the Bosphorus is traversed on a daily basis by thousands of cars, ferries, fishing boats and launches. Travelling in the famous public excursion ferry alongside massive tankers and cargo ships making their way from the Sea of Marmara to the Black Sea certainly makes a memorable day trip.

For those keen on a ferry encounter of a shorter kind, the services from Eminönü to Üsküdar and Kadıköy are perfect – particularly at sunset, when the grandiose silhouette of the Old City is thrown into relief against an orange-red or dusky pink sky. Yet another option is the enjoyable Haliç service, which leaves from Üsküdar and chugs up the Golden Horn to Eyüp every hour. On its jaunty progression it stops at Eminönü, Fener, Hasköy and Sütluce, making it an attractive option for sightseers wishing to visit parts of the city off the standard tourist trail.

See p111 for more information.

>6 İSTİKLAL CADDESİ

**WINE, DINE AND GALLERY-HOP ON AND AROUND
İSTİKLAL CADDESİ, THE HEART OF THE MODERN CITY**

İstiklal Caddesi (Independence Ave) is a perfect metaphor for 21st-
century Turkey. At one extremity is frantically busy Taksim Square,
the symbolic heart of modern İstanbul. Here a constant stream of
locals arrive by car, bus, funicular and metro to throw themselves
into the mayhem. At the other extremity is Galata, home to mean-
dering cobblestone lanes that have seen the comings and goings of
umpteen imperial powers. This part of town retains a slightly louche
and laid-back flavour, beckoning the traveller with its unexpected mix
of churches, mosques, shops, hotels and *hamams* (bathhouses). In
the long, bent boulevard in between, a constant stream of İstanbullus
browse in the boutiques and bookshops, gawk in the galleries and
party in umpteen *meyhanes* (taverns; see p82). As European as anything east of the Champs-Élysées, İstiklal (Independence) is either the
promise of Turkey's future or a mirage. Only time will tell which.

See p70 for more information.

>7 GALLERIES

GALLIVANT WITH THE IN-CROWD AT THE CITY'S AMAZING ART GALLERIES

Socially aspirational İstanbullus know that there's one foolproof way to build a public profile and keep up with the Joneses (or Koçs, as is the case here). All they need to do is build and endow an art gallery, preferably one dedicated to modern art. We can't explain why the botox-and-bling brigade has recently taken to culture with such alacrity, but this is indeed the case. And though bemused, we certainly don't wish to be seen as unsupportive. In fact, we reckon this trend is the best thing to hit the city since the tulip bulb arrived. First cab off the rank was the Proje4L/Elgiz Museum of Contemporary Art in Levent (take a bow Mr Elgiz), closely followed by İstanbul Modern (p74) in Tophane (hats off to Mrs Eczıbaşı) and the Pera Museum (p75) in Beyoğlu (round of applause to Mr and Mrs Kıraç). And let's not forget the privately endowed universities, which are joining the fray with style and loads of substance – the Sakıp Sabancı Müzesi (p117) and Santralİstanbul (p123) are the two most prominent, but there are a number of others starting to strut their stuff. All of this is great news for the visitor, who can see world-class exhibitions in drop-dead-gorgeous surrounds complete with stylish gift shops and quality cafes. Some are even free – and you gotta love that.

>8 SÜLEYMANİYE MOSQUE

VISIT THE MOST MAGNIFICENT OTTOMAN IMPERIAL MOSQUE IN THE CITY

Dominating the Old City's skyline, Süleyman the Magnificent's most notable architectural legacy lives up to its patron's name. The fourth imperial mosque built in İstanbul, the Süleymaniye was designed by Mimar Sinan, the most famous of all imperial architects, and was built between 1550 and 1557. Though it's seen some hard times, restorations in 1956 and 2010 have seen it reclaim its original glory. It's one of the most popular mosques in the city, with worshippers rivalling the Blue Mosque's in number.

Set in a walled garden, the mosque has a three-sided forecourt featuring an attractive domed ablutions fountain and is surrounded with its original *külliye* (complex of religious buildings), including *medreses* (theological schools) and an *imaret* (soup kitchen), *han* (caravansarai), *dar-üş-şifa* (hospital) and *hamam*. The building is luminous inside and out – its light-filled interior is breathtaking in its size and pleasing in its simplicity, with some fine İznik tiles and gorgeous stained-glass windows. The exterior is graced with four minarets featuring 10 delicate *şerefes* (balconies).

When you visit, don't miss the cemetery, home to the tombs of Süleyman and his wife Haseki Hürrem Sultan (Roxelana). The tilework in both is superb. See p55 for more information.

>9 HAMAMS

SURRENDER TO THE STEAM IN A TURKISH BATH

In life, there aren't too many opportunities to wander seminaked through a 16th-century Ottoman monument. Unless you visit İstanbul, that is. The city's world-famous *hamams* (Turkish baths) offer a unique opportunity to immerse yourself in history, architecture, warm water and soap suds – all at the same time. Many of the imperial mosque complexes include a *hamam*, and there are innumerable examples of historic neighbourhood baths dotted throughout the streets of the Old City – most, alas, now derelict or converted to shopping centres. Exceptions include the famous Çemberlitaş Hamamı (pictured above; p56), built by command of Nur Banu Valide Sultan, wife of Selim the Sot and mother of Murat III; and the Cağaloğlu Hamamı (p40), commissioned by Sultan Mahmut I.

Modern equivalents including the luxe spa at The Four Seasons İstanbul on the Bosphorus hotel (p127) offer indulgent takes on the traditional *hamam* experience.

HIGHLIGHTS

>10 THE GOLDEN MILE

PARTY THROUGH THE NIGHT AT A GOLDEN MILE SUPERCLUB

Pack a glam ensemble and get ready to squander some serious lira, because İstanbul's superclubs are as famous for their hard-assed door staff and wallet-decimating bar prices as they are for their magnificent Bosphorus views. They're worth it, though. The sybaritic strip between Ortaköy and Kuruçeşme is home to a clutch of nightclubs that epitomise the word indulgence – here patrons enjoy luxe surrounds, wonderful food, perfectly executed cocktails and a passing parade of Armani-clad businessmen, models on the make, one-hit celebs and local lasses squeezed into diamante-decorated jeans so tight their reproductive futures must be in serious danger. Reina (p109, pictured above), Sortie (p109), Anjelique (p106) and Blackk (p107) are perfect spots to contemplate the excesses and contradictions of this extraordinary city and feel the beat of its decidedly over-excited pulse.

>İSTANBUL DIARY

There's a massive range of entertainment options in İstanbul. In fact, the only thing that you can't do in this town is get bored. During the warmer months, the city is awash with major arts festivals and music events, most of which are organised by the **İstanbul Foundation for Culture and Arts** (☎ 212-334 0700; www.iksv.org; Sadi Konuralp Caddesi 5, Şişhane). Tickets to most events are available from **Biletix** (☎ 216-556 9800; www.biletix.com). For a list of public holidays, see p154.

İNSANNEYLEYAŞAR?

International İstanbul Biennial (p23)

APRIL

International İstanbul Film Festival

www.iksv.org/film

If you're keen to view the best in Turkish film and bump into a few local film stars while doing so, this is the event to attend. Held early in the month in cinemas around town, it's hugely popular. The program includes retrospectives and recent releases from Turkey and abroad.

International İstanbul Tulip Festival

The tulip (*lale* in Turkish) is one of İstanbul's traditional symbols, and the local govern-ment celebrates this fact by planting over three million of them annually. These bloom in late March and early April each year, endowing almost every street and park with vivid spring colours and wonderful photo opportunities.

JUNE

Efes Pilsen One Love

www.pozitif-ist.com

This two-day music festival is held at one of İstanbul's hippest art venues, Santralİstanbul (see p123). International headline acts play everything from punk to pop, electronica to disco.

International İstanbul Music Festival

www.iksv.org/muzik

İstanbul's premier arts festival features an extensive program of opera, dance, orchestral concerts and chamber recitals.

JULY

International İstanbul Jazz Festival

www.iksv.org/caz

The number-one jazz festival in town is an intriguing hybrid of conventional jazz, electronica, world music and rock. It's not only for beret-clad jazz aficionados, with artists such as Norah Jones, Antony & the Johnsons and Robert Plant playing

Happy crowds at the Efes Pilsen One Love festival

Take the time to smell the flowers at the International İstanbul Tulip Festival (p22)

alongside jazz greats such as Freddy Cole and Mike Stern.

SEPTEMBER

International İstanbul Biennial

www.iksv.org/bienal

The city's major visual-arts shindig takes place from early September to early November in odd-numbered years. An international curator nominates a theme and puts together a cutting-edge program, which is then exhibited in glam venues around town, including most of the major public and commercial galleries.

Akbank Jazz Festival

www.akbanksanat.com

This boutique event in late September and early October features traditional and avant-garde jazz, as well as Middle Eastern fusions and a program of young jazz. Venues include Akbank Sanat (p71), Babylon (p91) and Nardis Jazz Club (p93). Artists include international guests and local favourites such as İlhan Erşahin, Aydın Esen and İmer Demirer.

İSTANBUL DIARY

Tap your feet in time at the International İstanbul Jazz Festival (p22)

NOVEMBER

Efes Pilsen Blues Festival

www.pozitif-ist.com

This long-running event tours nationally, keeping blues fans smiling and leaving an echo of boogie-woogie, zydeco and 12-bar blues from Adana to Trabzon. It stops for a two-day program in İstanbul. The main venue is the Lütfi Kırdar Convention & Exhibition Centre, a popular classical music venue, in Harbiye.

The striking architecture of Süleymaniye Mosque (p55)

ITINERARIES

Many visitors to İstanbul only experience Sultanahmet, and this is a real shame – to really get a feel for the city, cross the Galata Bridge at least once and make sure you take a ferry ride between Europe and Asia.

TWO DAYS

Start your sightseeing with Aya Sofya (p36) and its younger neighbour, the Blue Mosque (Sultan Ahmet Camii; p37). Spend the afternoon in the Grand Bazaar (Kapalı Çarşı; p52) and then cross the continents by taking a ferry from Eminönü to Kadıköy or Üsküdar. Finish the day by sampling the national dish (kebaps) at Develi (p65), Beyti (p65), Hamdi (p64) or Zinhan (p66).

Day two should be devoted to Topkapı Palace (Topkapı Sarayı; p39) and the İstanbul Archaeology Museums (p38). For dinner, make your way to Beyoğlu, where you can promenade along Istiklal Caddesi (p16) before partaking of meze, rakı (aniseed brandy) and good company at one of the *meyhanes* (taverns) on Nevizade or Sofyalı Sokaks (p80).

FOUR DAYS

Follow the two-day itinerary before hopping aboard a ferry on day three to explore the Bosphorus (p112) or the Golden Horn (Haliç; p118). Later in the afternoon, relax in one of the Old City's historic *hamams* (bathhouses; p40 or p56) before hitting Beyoğlu's bar scene (p87) and then kicking on to the superclubs on the Golden Mile (p106).

Day four should see you heading towards the western districts of the Old City to contemplate the extraordinarily beautiful Byzantine mosaics at the Chora Church (p68). Wind down with a fish dinner among the city's powerbrokers at Balıkçı Sabahattin (p44), followed by tea and a nargileh (water pipe) at Derviş Aile Çay Bahçesi (p49) or Café Meşale (p49).

İSTANBUL REVIVER

After your flight, take a brisk walk around the Hippodrome (p38), followed by a steamy massage at an Old City *hamam* (p40 or p56). After this you'll need belly fuel to get you through the rest of the day – stroll over

---

Top left Dip in at Vogue restaurant (p106) **Top right** The exquisite detail and colour of mosaics inside Chora Church (p68) **Bottom** The Bosphorus (p112), with the Ortaköy Mosque in the background, is one of İstanbul's main transport arteries

ITINERARIES

the Galata Bridge (Galata Köprüsü; p52) and have a terrific fish lunch at Tarıhı Karaköy Balık Lokantası (p86), followed by a decadent baklava hit at Karaköy Güllüoğlu (p84). Afterwards, walk up the hill past Galata Tower (Galata Kulesi; p74) to check out the Orientalist painting collection at the Pera Museum (p75). Stay in Beyoğlu for dinner (p80).

HOT İSTANBUL

The stifling summer heat of the city has long sent well-heeled İstanbullus scampering to the coast or their *yalıs* (waterfront residences). Those who stay put often cool down under the umbrellas of Set Üstü Çay Bahçesi (p47) in Gülhane Parkı, which overlooks the Bosphorus. Follow their lead in the morning, and then head underground to the Basilica Cistern (p37) or spend a few hours around the pool at the Çırağan Palace Hotel Kempinski (p105). In the evening, await the cool change while dining in style on the outdoor terraces of Mikla (p86), Teras Restaurant (p46) or Banyan (p105).

Drink vendor in front of the Blue Mosque (Sultan Ahmet Camii; p37) and its soaring minarets

FORWARD PLANNING

Three months before you go In the high tourist season (April to May and September to October) good accommodation is booked solid. For popular hotels, you'll need to book months in advance. The same applies to any type of accommodation during the Formula 1 Grand Prix in May/June.

One month before you go İstanbul's big-ticket festivals sell out fast – and for good reason. A night spent listening to a chamber orchestra in the historically rich and atmospheric Aya İrini (p48) will be a highlight of a lifetime, not just your holiday, so it's worth booking well ahead to ensure you get a ticket. Check www.iksv.org or www.pozitif-ist.com to see what's on.

Two weeks before you go Book a table for dinner at Mikla (p86), Changa (p83) or Hamdi Et Lokantası (p64). If you're keen to visit one of the superclubs along the Bosphorus (p106), do the same.

RAIN, HAIL OR SNOW

Start your wintry İstanbul day by admiring the mournfully beautiful sight of the city under snow. Journey up the Golden Horn (p118) to Eyüp and visit the Eyüp Sultan Mosque (p123) before making your way to Edirnekapı, where you can enjoy an Ottoman lunch at the elegant Asitane (p68) before popping next door to the Chora Church (p68). For dinner, head underground to the warmth of the atmospheric Sarnıç (p45) in Sultanahmet.

İSTANBUL FOR FREE

Put on your walking shoes and follow Divan Yolu (Ordu) Caddesi from the Hippodrome to the Grand Bazaar (p52). After getting lost in the bazaar's labyrinthine laneways, move on to the tranquil Süleymaniye and Şehzade Mehmet Mosques (p55 and p54) before admiring the magnificent Aqueduct of Valens (p52). Retrace your steps and head towards the fragrant mayhem of the Spice Bazaar (Mısır Çarşısı; p55), then cross the Galata Bridge (p52) and walk uphill to browse in the bookshops (p77) on İstiklal Caddesi. If it's a Thursday, finish by taking advantage of the free entry at İstanbul Modern (p74).

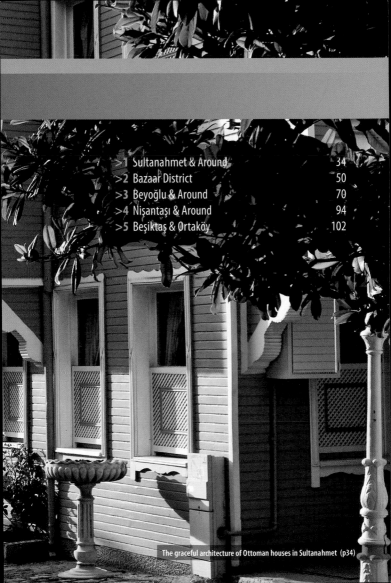

The graceful architecture of Ottoman houses in Sultanahmet (p34)

NEIGHBOURHOODS

İstanbul has more neighbourhoods than it has minarets (and that's a lot). Few locals can believably claim to have visited them all, so mere visitors have no chance at all.

Fortunately, this isn't a problem. Most of the headline sights are in a relatively compact area spanning either side of the romantically named Golden Horn (Haliç), the body of water that slices European İstanbul in two.

On one side of the Golden Horn is the historic peninsula, home to İstanbul's major tourist enclave, Sultanahmet. This is the heart of Old Byzantium and the area where visitors do the vast majority of their sightseeing.

West of Sultanahmet, up the famous Divan Yolu boulevard, is the bazaar district, which has at its centre the Grand Bazaar (Kapalı Çarşı). Behind the bazaar is the Süleymaniye Mosque, which graces the top of one of the Old City's hills and is one of the city's major landmarks. Down from the bazaar is the Golden Horn and the bustling transport hub of Eminönü.

From Eminönü, trams, taxis and a constant stream of pedestrians make their way over the Galata Bridge (Galata Köprüsü) to bohemian Beyoğlu, home to the vast majority of the city's bars and restaurants. The suburb's major landmark is manic Taksim Square, the symbolic centre of the modern city.

North of Taksim Square is the upmarket suburb of Nişantaşı, characterised by chic hotels, fashionable restaurants and glamorous boutiques. To its east, residential streets cascade down the hill to the Bosphorus shore and the suburbs of Beşiktaş and Ortaköy. Beşiktaş is home to lavish Dolmabahçe and Çirağan Palaces, both of which command spectacular views of the Bosphorus. To their north is the quaint waterside suburb of Ortaköy, nestled under the mighty Bosphorus Bridge.

Finally, no description of the city is complete without mentioning the Bosphorus strait, which joins the Black and Marmara Seas and divides Europe from Asia. It is the true lifeblood of this spectacularly sprawling, contrast-filled metropolis.

>SULTANAHMET & AROUND

Many visitors to İstanbul never make it out of Sultanahmet – and it's hardly surprising. After all, not many cities have such a concentration of sights, shops, hotels and eateries within easy walking distance.

Occupying the promontory that runs from the eastern side of Eminönü on the Golden Horn (Haliç) to Küçük Aya Sofya on the Sea of Marmara, this neighbourhood is centred on the Hippodrome. It incorporates a number of suburbs including Sultanahmet proper, where Aya Sofya and the Blue Mosque (Sultan Ahmet Camii) are located.

From late April to October, Sultanahmet's attractions draw huge crowds. Start early in the morning and don't visit on Sundays, when local tourists add to the crush.

SULTANAHMET & AROUND

◉ SEE

◉ AYA SOFYA

Sancta Sophia (Latin), Haghia Sofia
(Greek), Church of the Divine Wisdom
(English); ☎ 212-522 0989; Aya Sofya
Square; adult/child under 6yr TL20/free;
⏱ 9am-6pm Tue-Sun May-Oct, to 4pm
Nov-Apr; 🚇 Sultanahmet

The scaffolding-filled dome,
the din of the tour groups, the
occasional tacky exhibits and the
queues and touts waiting outside
drastically diminish the solem-
nity of a visit to this important
religious monument, but they
can't detract from the sheer
magnificence of the building.
An official guide costs TL50 for a
45-minute tour. See p12 for more
information.

◉ AYA SOFYA TOMBS

☎ Aya Sofya Türbeleri; Kabasakal
Caddesi; admission free; ⏱ 9am-7pm;
🚇 Sultanahmet

Part of the Aya Sofya complex, but
with an entrance on the road to
Topkapı Palace, these tombs are
the final resting places of sultans
Mehmed III, Selim II, Murad III,
İbrahim I, Mustafa I and their
families. Each of the buildings has
ornate interior decoration; the
tombs of İbrahim and Mustafa
are housed in Aya Sofya's original
baptistry, converted to a mau-
soleum in the 17th century but

Navigate the forest of columns at Basilica Cistern (p37)

GREAT PALACE OF BYZANTIUM

Constantine the Great built the Great Palace soon after he founded Constantinople in AD 324. Successive Byzantine leaders left their mark by adding to it, and the complex eventually consisted of hundreds of buildings enclosed by walls and set in terraced parklands stretching from the Hippodrome over to Aya Sofya and down the slope, ending at the sea walls and the Bucoleon Palace. The palace was finally abandoned after the Fourth Crusade sacked the city in 1204, and its ruins were pillaged and filled in after the Conquest, becoming mere foundations of much of Sultanahmet and Cankurtaran.

Various pieces of the Great Palace have been uncovered – many by budding hotelier 'archaeologists' – and an evocative stroll exploring the Byzantine substructure is a great way to spend an afternoon. The mosaic in the Great Palace Mosaic Museum (p38) once graced the floor of the complex, and excavations at the Sultanahmet Archaeological Park in Babıhümayun Caddesi, southeast of Aya Sofya, have been ongoing since 1998 but have stalled in recent years due to a heated and highly political debate that is being played out in local and national parliaments and through the media concerning plans by the neighbouring luxury Four Seasons Hotel to subsume some of the excavations into its huge new extension.

You can also view the remains of the Bucoleon Palace (Kennedy Caddesi), by the sea walls. For more information, check out www.byzantium1200.com, a project aimed at creating computer reconstructions of the Byzantine Monuments located in Istanbul as of year 1200 AD, or purchase a copy of the project's lavishly illustrated guidebook *Walking Thru Byzantium: Great Palace Region*.

closed for renovation when this book went to print.

◎ BASILICA CISTERN
Yerebatan Sarnıcı; ☎ 212-522 1259; www.yerebatan.com; Yerebatan Caddesi 13; admission TL10; ◷ 9am-7.30pm Apr-Sep, 9am-7.30pm Oct-Mar; ⊠ Sultanahmet
As if its wildly atmospheric forest of columns, carved Medusa heads and ghostly patrols of carp weren't drawcards enough, the cistern also has an intriguing history. Originally built to store water for the Great Palace of Byzantium, it fell into dis-use and was only rediscovered in the 16th century when a French archaeologist noticed local residents catching fish by lowering buckets through holes in their floors.

◎ BLUE MOSQUE
Sultan Ahmet Camii; Hippodrome; donation appreciated; ◷ closed during prayer times; ⊠ Sultanahmet
İstanbul's most photogenic building was the grand project of Sultan Ahmet I, whose tomb is located on the north side facing Sultanahmet Parkı. The mosque's wonderfully curvaceous exterior features six

minarets and is particularly striking when lit up at night. Thousands of blue İznik tiles adorn the interior and give the building its unofficial but commonly used name.

◉ GREAT PALACE MOSAIC MUSEUM

Büyüksaray Mozaik Müzesi; ☎ 212-518 1205; Torun Sokak; admission TL8; ◷ 9am-6pm Tue-Sun Jun-Oct, to 4.30pm Nov-May; ⓖ Sultanahmet

This museum was built to preserve and display a remarkable Byzantine mosaic featuring hunting and mythological scenes. Dating from Justinian's reign, the mosaic once graced a courtyard of the Great Palace of Byzantium (p37) and was uncovered by archaeologists in the mid-1950s during works at the Blue Mosque.

◉ HIPPODROME

Atmeydanı; ⓖ Sultanahmet

The Byzantine emperors loved nothing more than an afternoon at the chariot races, and this rectangular park was their venue of choice. In its heyday, the arena consisted of two levels of galleries, a central spine, starting boxes and the semicircular end known as the Sphendone (opposite). In its centre you'll find the granite **Obelisk of Theodosius**, brought from Egypt by the emperor in AD 390. Look for its carvings of Theodosius, his

Blue Mosque (p37) against a blue sky

wife, sons, state officials and bodyguards watching the action from the *kathisma* (imperial box).

◉ İSTANBUL ARCHAEOLOGY MUSEUMS

Arkeoloji Müzeleri; ☎ 212-520 7740; Osman Hamdi Bey Yokuşu, Gülhane Parkı; admission TL10; ◷ 9am-6pm Tue-Sun May-Sep, to 4pm Oct-Apr; ⓖ Gülhane

Put aside at least three hours for this superb complex, which houses a huge array of artefacts from the imperial collections. Highlights include the exquisite Alexander Sarcophagus, which depicts the Greek general and his army battling the Persians, and the extraordinary glazed-brick panels from the Ishtar gate of ancient Babylon. Archaeology buffs will appreciate the 'İstanbul Through the Ages' and 'In the Light of Day' exhibitions.

◉ MUSEUM OF TURKISH & ISLAMIC ARTS

**Türk ve İslam Eserleri Müzesi;
☎ 212-518 1805; Atmeydanı Sokak 46; admission TL10; ⏰ 9am-4.30pm Tue-Sun; 🚇 Sultanahmet**
This Ottoman palace on the Hippodrome was built for the influential İbrahim Paşa, childhood friend, brother-in-law and grand vizier of Süleyman the Magnificent. It's now home to a magnificent collection of artefacts representing almost every period and genre of Islamic art. The museum's collection of antique carpets is generally recognised as the best in the world, and the manuscripts and miniatures on display are equally impressive.

◉ SPHENDONE

Hippodrome; 🚇 Sultanahmet
The only remaining built section of the Hippodrome (opposite) hints at how monumental the arena was. The level of galleries that once topped this section was damaged during the Fourth Crusade and totally dismantled in the Ottoman period – many of the original columns were used in construction of the Süleymaniye Mosque (p55).

◉ TOPKAPI PALACE

Topkapı Sarayı; ☎ 212-512 0480; www .topkapisarayi.gov.tr/eng; Babıhümayun Caddesi; admission palace TL20, Harem TL15; ⏰ 9am-6pm Wed-Mon, Harem closes 5pm; 🚇 Sultanahmet or Gülhane
This is Turkey's number-one tourist attraction for good reason. Home to the Ottoman sultans for centuries, Topkapı has many treasures, including a gorgeous Harem, whimsical pavilions overlooking the Golden Horn (Haliç), and a museum full of

---

THE GREAT SİNAN

Libeskind might be revered, Gehry admired and Koolhaas worshipped, but none of today's star architects come close to having the influence over a city that Mimar Koca Sinan had over Constantinople during his 50-year career.

Born in 1497, Sinan was a recruit to the *devşirme,* the annual intake of Christian youths into the janissaries (Ottoman army), becoming a Muslim (as all such recruits did) and eventually taking up a post as a military engineer in the corps. Süleyman the Magnificent appointed him the chief of the imperial architects in 1538.

Sinan designed a total of 321 buildings, 85 of which are still standing in İstanbul. He died in 1588 and is buried in a self-built *türbe* (tomb) located on the north corner of the Süleymaniye Mosque, the building that many believe to be his greatest work.

jewel-encrusted treasures. Visiting the Harem is well worth the extra ticket price – buy one from the dedicated ticket office at its entrance. See p10 for more information.

🏃 DO

🏃 AMBASSADOR HOTEL SPA CENTER *Hamam*
☎ 212-512 0002; www.hotelambassador.com; Ticarethane Sokak 19; bath, scrub & massage TL75-118, remedial & aromatherapy massages TL49-118; 🕔 noon-11pm Mon-Fri, noon-midnight Sat & Sun; 🚇 Sultanahmet
Located in a modern hotel just off Divan Yolu, this small spa might lack atmosphere, but its bath and massage packages are excellent and you get the small *hamam* (bathhouse) all to yourself. We recommend paying the extra and adding the oil massage to its standard Turkish massage treatment. You can also book the *hamam* for private use (TL40 per person per hour).

🏃 CAĞALOĞLU HAMAMI
Hamam
☎ 212-522 2424; www.cagaloglu hamami.com.tr; Yerebatan Caddesi 34, Cağaloğlu; bath, scrub & massage TL78-98; 🕔 men 8am-10pm, women 8am-8pm; 🚇 Sultanahmet
The most beautiful of the city's *hamams*, historic Cağaloğlu

Hamamı offers separate baths for men and women and a range of bath services. You'll find a pleasant cafe as well as a shop selling quality olive-oil soap and other *hamam* accessories. Be warned that prices here are steep considering how quick and rudimentary the wash and massage is. See also p19 and p137.

🏃 URBAN ADVENTURES
Walking & Cultural Tours
☎ 212-512 7144; www.urbanadventures.com; 1st fl, Ticarethane Sokak 11; all tours €25; 🚇 Sultanahmet
This program of city tours includes a four-hour walk around Sultanahmet and the Bazaar District, and an evening spent enjoying dinner with a local family in their home.

🛍 SHOP

The best shopping in Sultanahmet is found in and around the Arasta Bazaar (B5). This historic arcade of shops was once part of the *külliye* (mosque complex) of the Blue Mosque and rents still go towards the mosque's upkeep. Some of Turkey's best-known rug and ceramic dealers have shops in the surrounding streets.

🛍 COCOON *Rugs, Textiles*
☎ 212-638 6271; www.cocoontr.com; Küçük Aya Sofya Caddesi 13; 🕔 8.30am-7.30pm; 🚇 Sultanahmet

There are so many rug and textile shops in İstanbul that choosing individual shops to recommend is incredibly difficult. We had no problem whatsoever in singling this one out, though. Felt hats, antique costumes and textiles from Central Asia are artfully displayed in one store, while rugs from Persia, Central Asia, the Caucasus and Anatolia adorn its neighbour. A third shop is in the Arasta Bazaar and another is in the Grand Bazaar (Kapalı Çarşı; p52).

☐ GALERİ KAYSERİ *Books*
☎ 212-512 0456; Divan Yolu (Ordu) Caddesi 11 & 58; 🕙 9am-9pm; 🚇 Sultanahmet

Twin shops almost opposite each other offer a range of English-language fiction and glossy books on İstanbul. The range is modest, but this is the best English-language bookshop this side of the Galata Bridge (Galata Köprüsü).

☐ İSTANBUL HANDICRAFTS MARKET
Ceramics & Handicrafts, Jewellery
İstanbul Sanat Çarşısı; ☎ 212-517 6782; Kabasakal Caddesi; 🕙 9am-6.30pm; 🚇 Sultanahmet

Tiny rooms surrounding the leafy courtyard of the 18th-century Cedid Mehmed Efendi Medresesi are home to this handicrafts centre. Artisan-made calligraphy,

embroidery, glassware, miniature paintings, ceramics and dolls are on offer.

☐ İZNİK CLASSICS & TILES
Ceramics
☎ 212-517 1705; www.iznikclassics .com; Arasta Bazaar 67, 73 & 161; 🕙 9am-8pm; 🚇 Sultanahmet

İznik Classics is one of the best places in town to source hand-painted collector-item ceramics made with real quartz and using metal oxides for pigments. Admire the range in the two shops and gallery in the Arasta Bazaar, in the Grand Bazaar (p60) store or in the newish outlet at Utangaç Sokak 17.

All styles of tiles at Arasta Bazaar

🖸 JENNIFER'S HAMAM
Textiles & Soap
☎ 212-518 0648; www.jennifers
hamam.com; 135 Arasta Bazaar;
🚇 Sultanahmet

This shop stocks *hamam* items
including towels, shawls, robes and
peştemalar (bath wraps). It also sells
natural soaps and rosense products
(natural rose hand and body products from Isparta).

🖸 KHAFTAN
Antiques & Art, Jewellery
☎ 212-458 5425; www.khaftan.com;
Nakilbent Sokak 33; 🕒 9am-8pm;
🚇 Sultanahmet

Owner Adnan Cakariz sells antique
Kütahya and İznik ceramics to
collectors and museums here
and overseas, so you can be sure
that the pieces he sells in his own
establishment are top-notch.
Gleaming Russian icons, delicate
calligraphy (old and new), ceramics, Karagöz puppets and contemporary paintings are all on show in
this gorgeous shop.

🖸 MEHMET ÇETİNKAYA
GALLERY *Rugs, Textiles*
☎ 212-517 6808; www.cetinkayagallery
.com; Tavukhane Sokak 7; 🕒 9.30am-
8.30pm; 🚇 Sultanahmet

When rug experts throughout
the country meet for their annual
shindig, this is one of the places
where they come to check out the

good stuff. There's a second shop
in the Arasta Bazaar.

🖸 MUHLİS GÜNBATTI *Textiles*
☎ 212-511 6562; Tevkifhane Sokak 12,
Cankurtaran; 🚇 Sultanahmet

The fact that this shop is located
opposite the posh Four Seasons
Hotel is a good indicator of the
quality and price of the antique
costumes and kaftans on offer
here. They're true collectors' items.

🖸 NAKKAŞ
Jewellery & Ceramics, Rugs
☎ 212-458 4702; Mimar Mehmet
Ağa Caddesi 39; 🕒 9am-7pm;
🚇 Sultanahmet

As well as pricey rugs and jewellery,
Nakkaş stocks an extensive range of
ceramics made by the well-regarded
İznik Foundation. One of the reasons
the place is so beloved of tour
groups is the beautifully restored
Byzantine cistern that's in the basement – make sure you have a peek.

🖸 YILMAZ İPEKÇİLİK
Textiles, Soap
☎ 212-638 4579; Ishakpaşa Caddesi 36,
Cankurtaran; 🕒 9am-9pm Mon-Sat,
3-9pm Sun; 🚇 Sultanahmet

Hand-loomed textiles made in a
family-run factory in Antakya are
on sale in this out-of-the-way shop.
Good-quality silk, cotton and linen
items at reasonable prices make it
worth the short trek.

Atilla Tuna
Byzantine history buff and tour guide with İstanbul Walks (p157)

When did your interest in Byzantine history and architecture start? Byzantine monuments enriched my childhood and made me passionately interested in their preservation. **Where can visitors see Byzantine monuments?** Most are located within the historical peninsula, but there are others in Kadiköy, the Princes Islands, Üsküdar and Galata. **Which are your favourites?** Definitely Aya Sofya (p12 and p36). It was a symbol of Byzantium and still it is. Also the Chora Church (p68), Basilica Cistern (p37), Theodosian Walls and Little Aya Sofya (p52). **Are they all in good condition?** Zeyrek Mosque is under threat but there is an ongoing project to restore the building. Little Aya Sofya has been restored. The City Walls, Aya Sofya and Chora Church are constantly undergoing restoration. But there is a complete underground Byzantine City under İstanbul that is under threat from ongoing development projects including the metro. For instance, the present municipality has given a permit to construct a hotel building on top of a Byzantine palace right by Aya Sofya!

🍴 EAT

You're certainly *not* spoiled for choice when it comes to eating well in Sultanahmet – most restaurants cater solely to travellers and couldn't give a toss about return customers. This means that they serve up food ranging from acceptable to appalling. We've listed exceptions to this sorry reality below.

🍴 BALIKÇI SABAHATTİN

Anatolian, Fish $$$

☎ 212-458 1824; www.balikcisabahattin.com; Seyit Hasan Koyu Sokak 1, Cankurtaran; ⏲ noon-midnight; 🚋 Sultanahmet

The limos outside Balıkçı Sabahattin pay testament to its enduring popularity with the city's establishment, who join hordes of cashed-up tourists in enjoying its limited menu of meze and fish. The food is excellent, though the service can be harried. You'll dine in a wooden Ottoman house or under a leafy canopy in the garden. It's wise to book ahead.

🍴 BUHARA RESTAURANT & OCAKBAŞI

Anatolian, Kebaps $$

☎ 212-527 5133; Nuruosmaniye Caddesi 7A, Cağaloğlu; ⏲ 11am-10pm; 🚋 Sultanahmet

If you're craving a kebap and haven't the time or inclination to

walk down the hill to Eminönü's Hamdi (p64) or Zinhan (p66), this unassuming eatery might be the solution. Management can be gruff and the servings are on the small side, but the quality of the meat is consistently good.

🍴 ÇİĞDEM PASTANESİ

Sweets, Börek $

☎ 212-526 8859; Divan Yolu (Ordu) Caddesi 62A, Alemdar; ⏲ 8am-11pm; 🚋 Sultanahmet

Çiğdem Pastanesi has been serving delicious treats to locals since 1961, and it's still going strong. The *ay çöreği* (pastry with a walnut, sultana and spice filling) is the perfect accompaniment to a cappuccino, and a cheese börek (filled savoury pastry) goes wonderfully well with a cup of tea or fresh juice.

🍴 COOKING ALATURKA

Anatolian $$

☎ 212-458 5919; www.cookingalaturka.com; Akbıyık Caddesi 72A; ⏲ lunch Mon-Sat & dinner Mon-Sat by reservation; 🚋 Sultanahmet; ✗

This great little restaurant is run by Dutch-born foodie Eveline Zoutendijk, who both knows and loves Anatolian food. She serves a set four-course menu (TL50) that changes daily according to what produce is in season and what's best at the local markets. Eveline says that she aims to create a little haven in the midst of carpet-selling frenzy and she has indeed done this. She also sells unusual and authentic produce such as homemade jams, pomegranate vinegar and *pekmez* (grape molasses), as well as a few Turkish cooking utensils.

🍴 KARADENİZ AİLE PIDE & KEBAP SOFRASI

Kebaps, Pide $
☎ 212-526 7202; Dr Emin Paşa Sokak 16; ⏱ 11am-11pm; 🚋 Sultanahmet

This long-timer situated off Divan Yolu serves a delicious *mercimek* (lentil soup) and is also a favourite for its pide (Turkish pizza). There are few frills, but the friendly service, convenient location and reasonable prices more than compensate. We think it's much better than the Karadeniz Aile Pide ve Kebap Salonu – the one with tables on the street corner – opposite.

🍴 PAŞAZADE

Kebaps, Pide $
☎ 212-526 7202; Dr Emin Paşa Sokak 16; ⏱ 11am-11pm; 🚋 Sultanahmet

Advertising itself as an Osmanlı mutfağı (Ottoman kitchen), Paşazade serves well-priced meals in its attractive streetside restaurant or on the rooftop terrace, which has great views. Portions

are large, the food is delicious and service is attentive.

🍴 SARNIÇ

Anatolian, International $$$
☎ 212-512 4291; Soğukçeşme Sokak; ⏱ 7-11pm; 🚋 Gülhane

It's not every day you get to dine in a wonderfully atmospheric candlelit Byzantine cistern, so we're listing Sarnıç despite the fact that its food can be disappointing. If he doesn't pop the question after a night out here, it's time to move on.

🍴 SEFA RESTAURANT

Anatolian, Kebaps $
☎ 212-520 0670; Nuruosmaniye Caddesi 17, Cağaloğlu; ⏱ 7am-5pm; 🚋 Sultanahmet

Locals rate this place near the Grand Bazaar highly, and after sampling the simple dishes on offer you'll understand why. You can order from an English-language menu or choose from the bain-marie. Try to arrive early-ish for lunch because many of the dishes run out by 1.30pm.

🍴 TARİHİ SULTANAHMET KÖFTECİSİ SELİM USTA

Köfte $
☎ 212-520 0566; Divan Yolu (Ordu) Caddesi 12; ⏱ 11am-11pm; 🚋 Sultanahmet

Don't get this establishment confused with the other *köfte* (meatball) places along this strip purporting to be the *meşhur* (famous) *köfte* restaurant – No 12 is the real McCoy. Locals flock here to eat the signature *köfte* served with white beans, pickled chillies and salad.

▦ TERAS RESTAURANT
Anatolian, Fish $$$
☎ 212-638 1370; Hotel Armada, Ahırkapı Sokak 24, Cankurtaran; ☾ 7-11pm; ◈ Sultanahmet
The chef at this upmarket hotel restaurant came up with an inspired idea when he devised his Turkish degustation menu (TL68). It features three courses of 'İstanbul cuisine' and is complemented by an excellent and affordable wine list. You can also order from the à la carte menu (the fish is particularly good). Book a terrace table with a view of the Blue Mosque.

▦ ZİYA ŞARK SOFRASI
Anatolian $$
☎ 212-512 7750; www.ziyasark.com.tr; Alemdar Caddesi 28; ☾ 8.30am-11pm; ◈ Gülhane
Located on the busy road between Eminönü and Sultanahmet just near the entrance to Gülhane Parkı, this eatery is popular with locals – always a good sign. The menu is varied (meze, kebaps and pides feature), everything is

fresh and well cooked, the decor is cheerful and the service is friendly. It's one of the best eating options in the area, albeit with an alcohol-free policy.

▼ DRINK
Or lack thereof. There are a few *çay bahçesiler* (tea gardens) in the Old City, but not many bars. If you want to go out on the tiles, make your way over the bridge to Beyoğlu.

▼ HOTEL NOMADE TERRACE
BAR *Hotel Bar*
☎ 212-513 8172; Ticarethane Sokak 15, Alemdar; ☾ noon-11pm; ◈ Sultanahmet
The intimate terrace of this boutique hotel overlooks Aya Sofya and the Blue Mosque. Settle down in a comfortable chair to enjoy a glass of wine, beer or freshly squeezed fruit juice. The only music that will disturb your evening's reverie is the Old City's signature sound of the call to prayer.

▼ KYBELE CAFE
Hotel Bar
☎ 212-511 7766; Yerebatan Caddesi 35, Alemdar; ☾ 3pm-1am; ◈ Sultanahmet
The lounge bar at this charming but vaguely eccentric hotel is chock-full of antique furniture, richly coloured rugs and old etchings and prints, but its signature

style comes courtesy of the hundreds of colourful glass lights hanging from the ceiling. It's a wonderfully atmospheric spot for a quiet drink.

☿ SET ÜSTÜ ÇAY BAHÇESİ
Tea Garden
Gülhane Parkı; ☽ **10am-11pm;**
☒ **Gülhane**
Locals adore this terraced tea garden. Every weekend they can be seen parading arm-in-arm through Gülhane Parkı to get here. Follow their example and enjoy *tost* (toasted sandwich) and a pot of tea while enjoying superb water views.

☿ SULTAN PUB *Pub*
☎ **212-511 5638; Divan Yolu (Ordu)**
Caddesi 2, Alemdar; ☽ **9.30pm-1am;**
☒ **Sultanahmet**
This local version of Ye Olde English Pub has been around for yonks. The 30-to-40ish crowds come for spectacular sunsets on the rooftop terrace or peerless people-watching from the sun-drenched streetside tables.

☿ YEŞİL EV *Hotel Bar*
☎ **212-517 6785; Kabasakal Caddesi 5;**
☽ **noon-10.30pm;** ☒ **Sultanahmet**
The elegant rear courtyard of this Ottoman hotel is a true oasis for

Downstairs at İstanbul Hotel Nomade (p46)

WORTH THE TRIP

Although most of İstanbul's noteworthy sights, shops, bars and eateries are on the European side of town, many locals prefer to live on the **Asian shore**, citing cheaper rents and a better standard of living. For others, the best thing about living on this side of town is the scenic ferry ride between the continents.

If you've got a spare few hours, you may want to explore **Kadıköy**, the site of the city's first colony. Although there's nothing to show of its historic beginnings and no headline sights, Kadıköy has a youthful, modern vibe that can be a welcome respite from the conservative Old City. There's a fantastic fresh produce market south of the ferry dock, in the middle of which is **Çiya Sofrası** (☎ 216-330 3190; Güneslibahçe Sokak 43; 🕙 11.30am-10pm; 🚢 Eminönü then ferry to Kadıköy), one of the city's best eateries. After sampling its magnificent cheap food, head to old-fashioned **Baylan Pastanesi** (☎ 216-336 2881; Muvakkithane Caddesi 19; 🕙 10am-10pm; 🚢 Eminönü then ferry to Kadıköy) for an excellent coffee. Then make your way to Kadife Sokak to check out its independent cinema, grunge boutiques and hugely popular bars.

North of Kadıköy is bustling **Üsküdar**, also established some two decades before Byzantium. Its clutch of mosques includes the commanding Sinan-designed **Atık Valide Mosque** (Çinili Camii Sokak, Tabaklar; donation requested; 🚢 Eminönü then ferry to Üsküdar, 🚌 12 or 12A from Kadıköy). It can be tricky to find the mosque on your own; a taxi from the ferry dock should cost no more than TL5 and is worth the price.

To the south of Üsküdar is the **Florence Nightingale Museum** (☎ 216-556 8161; fax 216-310 7929; Burhan Felek Caddesi, Selimiye; admission free; 🕙 9am-5pm Mon-Fri; 🚢 Harem or 🚌 12H, 1, 139 or 320 from Üsküdar). It was here, in the Selimiye Army Barracks, that Nightingale put into practice her innovative nursing methods. To visit, you need to fax a letter, including a photocopy of your passport photo page, requesting a visit and nominating a time. You'll need to do this some 48 hours before you wish to visit; include an İstanbul telephone number so that someone can respond.

those wanting to enjoy a quiet drink. In spring, flowers and blossoms fill every corner; in summer the fountain and trees keep the temperature down.

⭐ PLAY

⭐ AYA İRİNİ *Classical Music*
Haghia Eirene; First Court of Topkapı Palace; 🚇 **Gülhane or Sultanahmet**

Big-name classical music events make the most of the superb acoustics in this ancient church. If you're in the mood to sample some music while in town, be sure to wander by the information board outside to see if any concerts are scheduled during your visit, or check **Biletix** (www.biletix.com). It's a major venue for the International İstanbul Music Festival (p22).

⭐ DERVİŞ AİLE ÇAY BAHÇESİ
Nargileh Cafe, Tea Garden
Mimar Mehmet Ağa Caddesi;
🕐 9am-11pm Apr-Oct; 🚇 Sultanahmet
Locations don't come any better than this. Directly opposite the Blue Mosque, the Derviş' comfortable cane chairs and shady trees beckon patrons in need of a respite from the tourist queues. Situated close nearby, **Café Meşale** (☎ 212-518 9562; Arasta Bazaar, Utangaç Sokak, Cankurtaran; 🕐 24hr; 🚇 Sultanahmet) is equally welcoming and offers live Turkish music in the evening.

⭐ HODJAPAŞA CULTURE CENTER *Dance Performances*
☎ 212-511 4626; www.istanbuldervish .com, www.turkishdancenight.com; Hocapaşa Hamamı Sokak 5-9; 🕐 7.30pm Wed & Fri-Mon; 🚇 Sirkeci
Occupying a beautifully converted 550-year-old *hamam* near Eminönü, this cultural centre stages a one-hour whirling dervish performance for tourists (tickets adult/child under 15 TL40/25) on Wednesday, Friday, Saturday,

Sunday and Monday at 7.30pm, and a 70-minute performance of Turkish dances (TL50) every Tuesday and Thursday at 8pm and Saturday at 9pm. The Turkish dance night features everything from belly dance to traditional folk dance and modern interpretations; both it and the dervish performance are accompanied by live music. Book via the websites or ask your hotel to organise tickets.

⭐ YENİ MARMARA
Nargileh Cafe
☎ 212-516 9013; Çayıroğlu Sokak, Küçük Aya Sofya; 🕐 8am-midnight; 🚇 Sultanahmet
A neighbourhood teahouse that's always packed with locals sipping tea, puffing on nargilehs and playing backgammon, Yeni Marmara is as un-touristy as Sultanahmet gets. In winter, the heat from a wood stove stokes conversation on comfy lounges; in summer, patrons shoot the breeze on the rear terrace overlooking the Sea of Marmara.

>BAZAAR DISTRICT

In the Ottoman era, ships from the far reaches of the empire and beyond travelled to the capital, bringing goods that were sold in the Grand Bazaar (Kapalı Çarşı) and Spice Bazaar (Mısır Çarşısı) and stored in *hanlar* (caravanserais) in the vast market district that spills northwards from the Grand Bazaar to Eminönü. Today, this area is still characterised by its mercantile madness.

To the west of the Grand Bazaar on Yeniçeriler Caddesi (the continuation of Divan Yolu) is Beyazıt Square, officially known as Hürriyet Meydanı, a bustling meeting place for shoppers and students from nearby İstanbul University. Behind the university is the grand Süleymaniye Mosque, which has given its name to the surrounding suburb. See p14 for more information about the district.

BAZAAR DISTRICT

🔵 SEE
Aqueduct of Valens	**1**	A2
Çemberlitaş	**2**	D4
Galata Bridge	**3**	D1
Grand Bazaar	**4**	C4
Little Aya Sofya	**5**	D6
New Mosque	**6**	D2
Rüstem Paşa Mosque	**7**	C2
Şehzade Mehmet Mosque	**8**	A3
Sokollu Şehit Mehmet Paşa Mosque	**9**	D5
Spice Bazaar	**10**	D2
Süleymaniye Mosque	**11**	B2
Valide Han	**12**	C3
Zeyrek Mosque	**13**	A2

🟢 DO
Çemberlitaş Hamamı	**14**	D4

🟠 SHOP
Ali Muhiddin Hacı Bekir	**15**	D2
Arifoğlu	(see 10)	
Arslan Baharat	(see 10)	
Design Zone	**16**	D4
Kurukahveci Mehmet Efendi	**17**	C2
Malatya Pazarı	(see 10)	
Sofa	**18**	D4
Sûfi	**19**	D2
Vakko İndirim	**20**	D3

🍴 EAT
Bab-ı Hayat	**21**	D2
Hafız Mustafa Şekerlemeleri	**22**	D2
Hamdi Et Lokantası	**23**	C2
İmren Lokantası	**24**	D5
Namlı	**25**	D2
Sur Ocakbası	**26**	A2
Tarihi Süleymanıyeli Fasülyeci Erzincanlı Alı Baba	**27**	B2
Zeyrekhane	**28**	A1
Zinhan Kebap House at Storks	**29**	C2

🍸 DRINK
Coffee World	**30**	D4
Fes Cafe	**31**	D4
Vefa Bozacısı	**32**	A3

✴ PLAY
Erenler Aile Çay Bahçesi	33	C4
İesam Lokalı	34	C4
Lale Bahçesi	35	B2
Şafak Sinemaları	36	D4
Türk Ocağı Kültür ve Sanat Merkezi İktisadi İşletmesi Çay Bahçesi	37	D4

👁 SEE

👁 AQUEDUCT OF VALENS

**Map p51; Atatürk Bulvarı;
🚇 Laleli-Üniversite**

Rising majestically over the traffic on busy Atatürk Bulvarı, this limestone aqueduct is one of the city's most distinctive landmarks. Commissioned by Emperor Valens in AD 373, it was part of an elaborate system linking more than 400km of water channels, some 30 bridges and over 100 cisterns within the city walls, making it one of the greatest hydraulic engineering achievements of ancient times.

👁 ÇEMBERLİTAŞ

**Map p51; Divan Yolu (Ordu) Caddesi,
Çemberlitaş; 🚇 Çemberlitaş**

Commonly overlooked by travellers and locals alike, this simple banded column is actually one of the city's most ancient and significant monuments, erected by Constantine to celebrate the dedication of Constantinople as capital of the Roman Empire in AD 330. It recently underwent a long and much-needed renovation.

👁 GALATA BRIDGE

**Map p51; Galata Köprüsü; 🚇 Karaköy
or Eminönü**

Nothing is quite as evocative as walking across the Galata Bridge at sunset, when the mosques atop the seven hills of the city

are thrown into relief against a soft red-pink sky and the smell of apple tobacco wafts up from the nargileh cafes below. This is also the best spot in the city to view the ferries plying the waters of the Golden Horn (Haliç).

👁 GRAND BAZAAR

**Map p51; Kapalı Çarşı; 🕙 8.30am-
7.30pm Mon-Sat; 🚇 Beyazıt-Kapalı
Çarşı**

When Mehmet the Conqueror laid the foundation stone for the bazaar, he planted the seed for the most important marketplace in the Ottoman Empire. His original *bedesten* (vaulted market enclosure), now an antiques and curios hall, spread and engulfed surrounding *hanlar,* creating the chaotic shopping crush you see today. See p59 for shopping suggestions.

👁 LITTLE AYA SOFYA

**Map p51; Küçük Aya Sofya; Küçük Aya
Sofya Caddesi, Küçük Aya Sofya;
donation requested; 🚇 Sultanahmet
or Çemberlitaş**

After being listed on the **World Monuments Fund** (www.wmf.org) register of endangered buildings, this gorgeous example of Byzantine architecture has recently been restored and is looking terrific. Built by Justinian and Theodora between AD 527 and 536 as the

GRAND BAZAAR

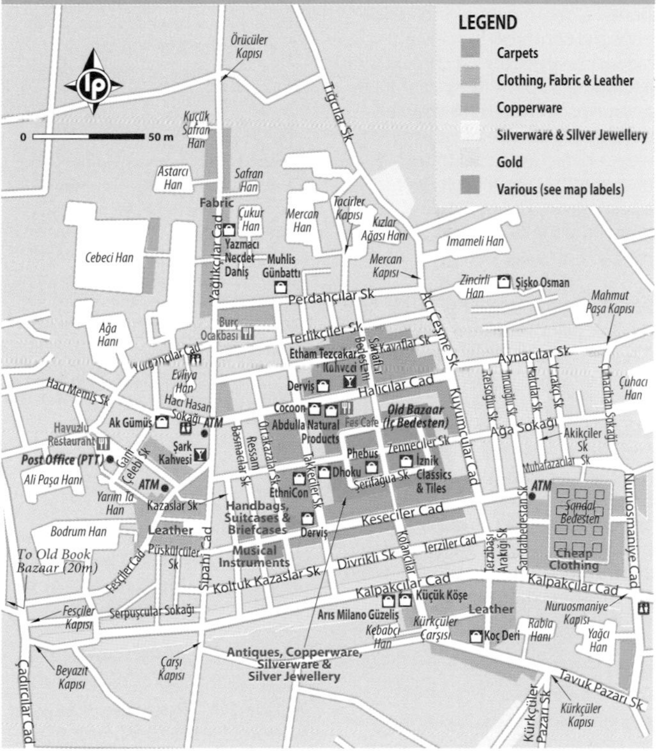
LEGEND
Carpets
Clothing, Fabric & Leather
Copperware
Silverware & Silver Jewellery
Gold
Various (see map labels)
0
50 m
Örücüler Kapısı
Küçük Safran Han
Astarcı Han
Safran Han
Fabric
Çukur Han
Yazmacı Necdet Daniş
Muhlis Günbattı
Mercan Han
Tacirler Kapısı
Kızlar Ağası Hanı
Mercan Kapısı
Imameli Han
Zincirli Han
Şişko Osman
Mahmut Paşa Kapısı
Cebeci Han
Ağa Hanı
Tığcılar Sk
Yağlıkçılar Cad
Perdahçılar Sk
Burç Ocakbaşı
Terlikçiler Sk
Etham Tezçakar Kahvecİ
Kavaflar Sk
Sarraflar
Acı Çeşme Sk
Aynacılar Sk
Çuhacı Han
Çuhacıhan Sokağı
Evliya Han
Hacı Memiş Sk
Hacı Hasan Sokağı
Derviş
Halıcılar Cad
Cocoon
Old Bazaar (İç Bedesten)
Fes Cafe
Abdulla Natural Products
Ak Gümüş
ATM
Havuzlu Restaurant
Post Office (PTT)
Şark Kahvesi
Ali Paşa Hanı
Kuyumcular Cad
Ağa Sokağı
Akikçiler Sk
Muhafazacılar Sk
Zenneciler Sk
Phebus
Dhoku
İznik Classics & Tiles
Serifağua Sk
Ressam
Ortakazalar Sk
Takkeciler Sk
Basmacılar Sk
EthniCon
Yarım Ta Han
Kazaslar Sk
Handbags, Suitcases & Briefcases
Keseciler Cad
Nuruosmaniye Cad
Sandal Bedesten
Cheap Clothing
Bodrum Han
Leather
Püskülcüler Sk
Sipahi Cad
Musical Instruments
Divrikli Sk
Terziler Cad
Kolancılar
Fesçiler Cad
To Old Book Bazaar (20m)
Koltuk Kazaslar Sk
Kalpakçılar Cad
Küçük Köşe
Leather
Nuruosmaniye Kapısı
Fesçiler Kapısı
Serpuşçular Sokağı
Arıs Milano Güzeliş
Kebabçı Han
Kürkçüler Çarşısı
Koç Deri
Rabia Hanı
Yağcı Han
Antiques, Copperware, Silverware & Silver Jewellery
Beyazıt Kapısı
Çarşı Kapısı
Çadırcılar Cad
Tavuk Pazarı Sk
Kürkçüler Pazarı Sk
Kürkçüler Kapısı

Church of St Sergius and Bacchus, it was converted into a mosque around AD 1500. There's a tranquil *çay bahçesi* (tea garden) in the forecourt.

NEW MOSQUE

Map p51; Yeni Cami; Yenicami Meydanı Sokak, Eminönü; donation appreciated; Eminönü

In 1597, Valide Sultan Safiye, mother of Mehmet III, commissioned a new mosque and *külliye* (mosque complex) in the commercial heart of the city. Residents (including a community of Karaite Jews, who were sent to the newly developing suburb of Hasköy) were evicted and a building program that would last 66 years commenced. The mosque is now one of the major adornments to the Old City's skyline.

☾ RÜSTEM PAŞA MOSQUE

Map p51; Hasırcılar Caddesi, Rüstempaşa; donation appreciated; ☒ Eminönü
This little-visited mosque is a gem. Designed by Sinan (see p39) and built by Rüstem Paşa, son-in-law and grand vizier of Süleyman the Magnificent, it's a showpiece of the very best Ottoman architecture and İznik tilework, albeit on a small scale. Climb the stairs to access the terrace and colonnaded porch, from where you can enter the mosque itself.

☾ ŞEHZADE MEHMET MOSQUE

Map p51; Mosque of the Prince; Şehzadebaşı Caddesi, Kalenderhane; donation requested; ☒ Laleli-Üniversite
Süleyman the Magnificent commissioned Sinan to design this mosque in memory of his son Mehmet, who died of smallpox at

the age of 22. It was completed in 1548 and is noteworthy for its delicate minarets and attractive garden setting. From here, you can take the Atatürk Bulvarı underpass west and follow the Aqueduct of Valens into the conservative suburbs of Fatih and Zeyrek.

☾ SOKULLU ŞEHİT MEHMET PAŞA MOSQUE

Map p51; Şehit Mehmet Paşa Yokuşu, Küçük Aya Sofya; donation appreciated; ☒ Sultanahmet or Çemberlitaş
This diminutive mosque was designed by Sinan in 1571, when he was at the height of his architectural career. Its interior is beautifully proportioned and

features some of the finest İznik tiles ever made. Students of the *medrese* (theological school) would have lived and studied in the small rooms surrounding the courtyard.

◎ SPICE BAZAAR
Map p51; Mısır Çarşısı, Egyptian Market; Eminönü; ⏱ 8am-7pm Mon-Sat; 🚇 Eminönü

Vividly coloured pyramids of spices and ornate displays of jewel-like *lokum* (Turkish delight) provide eye candy for the thousands of tourists who tramp through this Ottoman marketplace every day. It's also a regular shopping spot for the city's best chefs, who come here to buy nuts, dried fruit and spices. Don't be afraid to do as the locals do – try before you buy and also compare prices with shops on neighbouring Hasırcılar Caddesi.

◎ SÜLEYMANİYE MOSQUE
Map p51; Prof Sıddık Sami Onar Caddesi, Süleymaniye; donation requested; 🚇 Beyazıt-Kapalı Çarşı

The Süleymaniye, which sits atop one of the city's seven hills, was the crowning glory of Sinan's prodigious architectural output and is widely acknowledged to be the most important imperial mosque in İstanbul. It retains its original *medrese, imaret* (soup kitchen;

now the Dârüzziyafe Restaurant, a good spot for a tea or coffee stop) and still-functioning *hamam*. See also p18.

◎ VALİDE HAN
Map p51; Çakmakçılar Yokuşu, Mercan; 🚇 Beyazıt-Kapalı Çarşı

Built in 1651, this is the largest *han* in the city. It's grubby, but intact enough to give an idea of what it must have been like in its Ottoman heyday. Then, snorting animals would have been tethered in the courtyard, the rooms above would vibrate with the snores of up to 3000 merchants, and the storerooms would have been loaded with fragrant spices and other exotic goods.

ALL HAIL THE HAN

An Ottoman *han* is basically a Persian-style caravanserai, with the addition of workshops and storage space for traders' wares. They were built by rich merchants at the edges of a bazaar so that caravans could unload and trade their spices, furs, silks and slaves right in the bazaar precincts. The *hanlar* were typically two- to three-storey arcaded buildings backed by small rooms for accommodation and storage, with the courtyard housing the animals. Although *hanlar* are found all over Turkey, the concentration in İstanbul's bazaar district is unrivalled, a testament to the city's importance as a trading-route hub.

ZEYREK MOSQUE

**Map p51; Church of the Pantocrator;
İbadethane Sokak, Zeyrek;**
Aksaray

This mosque was originally part
of an important Byzantine sanctu-
ary comprising two churches,
a chapel and a monastery. It's
presently in a deplorable state of
disrepair, and is currently closed
to the public while it waits for
long-overdue restoration works
to commence. In its grounds is
the restaurant Zeyrekhane (p66),
which has a terrace with spectacular views over the Golden
Horn.

DO

ÇEMBERLİTAŞ HAMAMI
Hamam

**Map p51; ☎ 212-522 7974; www
.cemberlitashamami.com.tr; Vezir Hanı
Caddesi 8, Çemberlitaş; bath, scrub
& massage TL55; 6am-midnight;
Çemberlitaş**

Designed by Sinan in 1584,
Çemberlitaş now functions as a
tourist *hamam* offering standard
bath treatments as well as facials
and oil massages. Like Cağaloğlu
Hamamı (p40), it's a double
hamam, with separate baths for
men and women. The original

A visit to Ali Muhiddin Haci Bekir will delight your tastebuds – and your dentist (p57)

TURKISH DELIGHT

Ali Muhiddin Hacı Bekir was the most famous of all Ottoman confectioners. In 1777 he came to İstanbul from the mountain town of Kastamonu in the north of present-day Turkey. He opened a shop in the Old City where he concocted delicious boiled sweets and the translucent jellied jewels known to Turks as *lokum* and to the rest of the world as Turkish delight. His products became so famous throughout the city that his sweetshop empire (below) grew, and his name became inextricably linked in the minds of İstanbullus with authentic and delicious *lokum*.

As well as enjoying *sade* (plain) *lokum*, you can buy it made with *cevizli* (walnut) or *şam fıstıklı* (pistachio), or flavoured with *portakallı* (orange), *bademli* (almond) or *roze* (rose water). Try a *çeşitli* (assortment) to sample the various types.

camekan (dressing room) is for men only, but an impressive new version for females has recently opened within the walls of the original building. Tips are covered by the admission prices here, which is a blessed relief. See also p19 and p137.

🔲 SHOP

🔲 ABDULLA NATURAL PRODUCTS
Textiles, Soap

Map p53; ☎ 212-527 3684; Halıcılar Caddesi 62, Grand Bazaar; ⏱ 8.30am-7.30pm Mon-Sat; 🚇 Beyazıt-Kapalı Çarşı

Make sure you keep your luggage allowance in mind when browsing through the wares at this stylish shop. It sells handmade woollen throws from eastern Turkey, top-quality cotton bed and bath linen, and beautifully packaged olive-oil soap.

🔲 AK GÜMÜŞ
Handicrafts, Jewellery

Map p53; ☎ 212-526 0987; www.ak-gumus.com; Gani Çelebi Sokak 8, Grand Bazaar; ⏱ 8.30am-7.30pm Mon-Sat; 🚇 Beyazıt-Kapalı Çarşı

Specialising in Central Asian tribal arts, this delightful store stocks an array of felt toys and hats, as well as jewellery and other objects made using coins and beads.

🔲 ALİ MUHİDDİN HACI BEKİR
Food & Drink

Map p51; ☎ 212-522 0666; www.hacibekir.com.tr; Hamidiye Caddesi 83, Eminönü; ⏱ 9am-8pm Mon-Sat; 🚇 Eminönü

It's obligatory to sample *lokum* (see the boxed text, above) while in İstanbul, and one of the best places to do so is at this historic shop, which has been operated by members of the same family for over 200 years. There are other branches in Beyoğlu (p78) and Kadıköy.

◩ ARIFOĞLU
Food & Drink

Map p51; ☎ 212-522 6612; Mısır Çarşısı 31 & 59 (Spice Bazaar), Eminönü; ☼ 8am-7pm Mon-Sat; 🚇 Eminönü
This is the ancient-remedy power-house of the city, with well-versed staff who can find a lotion or po-tion for everything from stomach aches to haemorrhoids.

◩ ARIS MILANO GÜZELIŞ
Jewellery

Map p51; ☎ 212-527 6648; Kalpakçılar Caddesi 103, Grand Bazaar; ☼ 8.30am-7.30pm Mon-Sat; 🚇 Beyazıt-Kapalı Çarşı
When this family-run business started trading here in 1957, it was one of only 10 or so jewellery shops in the Grand Bazaar. The Güzeliş family have been making

jewellery to order using every gold grade and every conceivable gem since this time, and have built a trusted reputation in the process.

◩ ARSLAN BAHARAT
Food & Drink

Map p51; ☎ 212-522 9589; Mısır Çarşısı 39 (Spice Bazaar), Eminönü; ☼ 8am-7pm Mon-Sat; 🚇 Eminönü
A good range of spices keeps most travellers happy, but serious shoppers know that this spot has the city's best range of rare natural aromatics such as musk and amber. It also stocks saffron at good prices.

◩ COCOON *Rugs, Textiles*
Map p53; www.cocoontr.com; Halıcılar Caddesi 42, Grand Bazaar; ☼ 8.30am-7.30pm Mon-Sat; 🚇 Beyazıt-Kapalı Çarşı

CARPET- & KİLİM-BUYING TIPS
Turkey is famous for its beautiful carpets and kilims (pileless woven rugs), and the range in İstanbul is unrivalled. To ensure you get a good buy, you may want to follow some of these guidelines:
> Spend time visiting shops and comparing prices and quality. It's also worth taking a look in the shops at home before you leave.
> A good-quality, long-lasting carpet or kilim should be 100% wool. Is the wool fine and shiny, with signs of the natural oil? Can you see fine, frizzy fibres common to wool on the back? Recycled or cheap wool feels scratchy and has no sheen, and the cheapest carpets may be made from *floş* (mercerised cotton).
> Beware the salespeople who assert their carpets are coloured with natural dyes, as chemi-cal dyes have been the main method of colouring for decades. There is nothing wrong with chemical dyes, but natural dyes and colours tend to be preferred and therefore fetch higher prices. Both natural and chemical dyes fade (despite what the salesperson might tell you).
> If you see the colours are lighter on the surface than in the pile, it's often an indication that the surface has faded in the sun, but not necessarily that it is an antique.

BARGAINING BASICS

Bargaining is the modus operandi in İstanbul's bazaars, and to do it effectively there are a few rules to keep in mind:

> Take your time. The shopkeepers here enjoy the ritual of bargaining and will give their best offers to shoppers who appear to be enjoying themselves, who are polite and who take their shopping seriously.

> Do your homework. Look closely at similar goods in several shops, assess their quality and ask their price but don't make any offers. In this way you can ascertain the relative worth of the item you have chosen.

> Play the game. When you eventually identify the item you want, ask the shopkeeper for his price. He'll always quote a figure that is inflated, and you should respond by offering an amount between 25% and 50% lower. After laughing or pretending to be mortally offended, he'll usually counter with a price somewhere between his original quote and your offer.

> Follow through. The bargaining process will usually go back and forth several times before a price is agreed upon and the transaction is completed. The shopkeeper will never sell for a price that is less than the item is worth to him, and you should never pay more than you feel the item is worth to you. One more important point: if you make an offer, it is extremely bad form to change your mind after it has been accepted.

This small branch of the very stylish Sultanahmet-based textile and rug business (see p40) specialises in jewellery and items made from felt.

🏠 **DERVİŞ**
Textiles, Soap
Map p53; ☎ 212-514 4525; www .dervis.com; Keseciler Caddesi 33-35, Grand Bazaar; ⏰ 8.30am-7.30pm Mon-Sat; 🚇 Beyazıt-Kapalı Çarşı
At Derviş gorgeous raw cotton and silk *peştemalar* (bath towels) share shelf space with traditional Turkish dowry vests and engagement dresses. If these garments don't

take your fancy, the pure olive-oil soaps and old *hamam* bowls are sure to step into the breach. There is another store at Halıcılar Caddesi 51.

🏠 **DESIGN ZONE** *Jewellery, Art*
Map p51; ☎ 212-527 9285; www .designzone.com.tr; Shop 4, Ali-baba Türbe Sokak 21, Nuruosmaniye; ⏰ 10am-6pm Mon-Sat; 🚇 Çemberlitaş
Contemporary Turkish designers show and sell their work in this attractive boutique, which has stock catering for all budgets. Look out for the super-stylish jewellery and handcrafted *hamam*-bowl sets created by owner Özlem Tuna (p61).

☐ DHOKU *Rugs*
Map p53; ☎ 212-527 6841; Takkeciler Sokak 58-60, Grand Bazaar; ☽ 8.30am-7.30pm Mon-Sat; ☒ Beyazıt-Kapalı Çarşı

One of a new generation of rug stores in the Bazaar, Dhoku (meaning 'texture') designs and sells contemporary kilims (pileless woven rugs) featuring attractive modernist designs. The same people run the **EthniCon store** (www .ethnicon.com), opposite.

☐ İZNİK CLASSICS & TILES *Ceramics*
Map p53; ☎ 212- 520 2568; www .iznikclassics.com; Şerifağa Sokak 18-21, Grand Bazaar; ☽ 8.30am-7.30pm Mon-Sat; ☒ Beyazıt-Kapalı Çarşı

A branch of the Arasta Bazaar ceramics shop (p41).

☐ KOÇ DERİ *Leather*
Map p53; ☎ 212-527 5553; Kürkçüler Çarşısı 22-46, Grand Bazaar; ☽ 8.30am-7.30pm Mon-Sat; ☒ Beyazıt-Kapalı Çarşı

Fancy a leather jacket or coat? Koç is bound to have something that suits. It's one of the bazaar's busiest and longest-running stores.

☐ KÜÇÜK KÖŞE *Leather*
Map p53; ☎ 212-513 0335; Kalpakçılar Caddesi 89-91, Grand Bazaar; ☽ 8.30am-7.30pm Mon-Sat; ☒ Beyazıt-Kapalı Çarşı

If you want a Kelly or a Birkin but can't afford Hermès, try here. It sells good-quality copies of designer bags for a fraction of the price.

☐ KURUKAHVECİ MEHMET EFENDİ *Food & Drink*
Map p51; ☎ 212-511 4262; www .mehmetefendi.com; Tahmis Sokak 66, Rüstempaşa; ☽ 9am-6.30pm Mon-Fri, 9am-2pm Sat; ☒ Eminönü

Caffeine addicts are regularly spotted queuing outside this flagship store of İstanbul's most famous coffee purveyor. You can join them in getting a fix of the freshest beans in town, or purchase a cute little set of two signature coffee cups, a coffee pot and coffee.

☐ MALATYA PAZARI *Food & Drink*
Map p51; ☎ 212-520 0440; Mısır Çarşısı 44 (Spice Bazaar), Eminönü; ☽ 8am-7pm Mon-Sat; ☒ Eminönü

The city of Malatya in central-eastern Turkey is famed for its apricots, and these three shops on the intersection (all with the same owner) stock the cream of the crop, dried both naturally and chemically. The other quality dried fruit and nuts eclipse all others in this bazaar.

☐ MUHLİS GÜNBATTI *Textiles*
Map p53; ☎ 212-511 6562; Perdahçılar Sokak 48, Grand Bazaar; ☽ 8.30am-7.30pm Mon-Sat; ☒ Beyazıt-Kapalı Çarşı

Özlem Tuna
Jewellery designer and owner of Design Zone (p59).

Why did you choose to open your store near the Grand Bazaar? I love the ancient area of Nuruosmaniye – it's full of lively energy and is so culturally rich. **Do you have favourite places in the bazaar?** I love the textiles at Yazmacı Necdet Daniş (p63) and I enjoy eating kebaps from Burç Ocakbaşı (☎ 212-527 1516; near Terlikçiler Sokak, off Yağlıkçılar Caddesi; kebaps TL7-18; ⏰ 8.30am-7pm Mon-Sat). **Is it hard for a female to work as a jeweller in Turkey?** Yes, most jewellers are still male. Things are changing, though. I have recently become the first woman to join the İstanbul Jewellery Council. **Are there many jewellers working around the Grand Bazaar?** The big jewellery manufacturers have moved out of the city centre, but some small ateliers are still based here. İstanbul's artisan traditions and training are intangible heritage – we must protect them and make sure that these ateliers and their *ustas* (masters) stay.

This famous store specialises in Uzbeki *suzani*, fabric made from fine cotton embroidered with silk. It's sold throughout İstanbul, but the range and quality here is unbeatable. There's a second shop in Sultanahmet (p42).

PHEBUS *Jewellery*
Map p53; ☎ 212-520 7932; Şerifağa Sokak 122, Cevahir Bedesten, Grand Bazaar; 🕙 8.30am-7.30pm Mon-Sat; 🚇 Beyazıt-Kapalı Çarşı

Enter this tiny shop in the heart of the bazaar to see the owner creating his attractive gold jewellery, some of which references Byzantine designs. You can choose something from the stock or have a piece custom-made.

ŞİŞKO OSMAN *Rugs*
Map p53; ☎ 212-528 3548; www .siskoosman.com; Zincirli Han 15, Grand Bazaar; 🕙 8.30am-7.30pm Mon-Sat; 🚇 Beyazıt-Kapalı Çarşı

The Osman family, including Şişko Osman (Fat Osman), runs one of the oldest and most respected rug dealerships. Even if you're not after a rug, it's well worth visiting just to view the gorgeous Zincirli Han, which the Osman shops have almost entirely colonised.

SOFA
Antiques & Jewellery, Art & Prints
Map p51; ☎ 212-520 2850; www .kashifsofa.com; Nuruosmaniye Caddesi 85, Nuruosmaniye; 🕙 9.30am-7pm Mon-Sat; 🚇 Çemberlitaş

In a pedestrian mall popular with cashed-up cruise-shippers, this atmospheric and welcoming shop offers quality prints, ceramics, calligraphy, curios and even contemporary paintings. The gold jewellery inspired by Ottoman and Byzantine designs is exquisite.

SÛFÎ *Jewellery, Homewares*
Map p51; ☎ 0212-527 4437; www. sufiart.net; Mısır Çarşısı 45 (Spice Bazaar), Eminönü; 🕙 8am-7pm Mon-Sat; 🚇 Eminönü

After wandering past the wealth of sweets, nuts, fruits and aromatics on display in the bustling Spice Bazaar, you may want to check out the tempting and eclectic range of jewellery, ceramics and homewares on offer here.

ANTIQUES, ANYONE?
Those seeking out authentic Ottoman souvenirs should visit the **Horhor Antique Market** (Horhor Antikacılar Çarşısı; off Map p51; Kırma Tulumba Sokak, Aksaray; 🕙 vary according to shop; 🚇 Aksaray), where the city's serious collectors congregate. This decrepit building in Aksaray is home to five floors of shops selling antiques, curios and bric-a-brac of every possible description, quality and condition.

📷 VAKKO İNDİRİM *Clothing*

Map p51; ☎ 212-522 8941; Sultan Hamamamı Sokak 24, Eminönü; ⏲ 9.30am-6pm Mon-Sat; 🚇 Eminönü

This remainder outlet of İstanbul's most glamorous department store should be on the itinerary of all bargain hunters. Top-quality men's and women's clothing (often apparel that has been designed and made in Italy) is sold here for a fraction of its original price.

📷 YAZMACI NECDET DANIŞ *Textiles*

Map p53; ☎ 212-526 7748; Yağlıkçılar Caddesi 57, Grand Bazaar; ⏲ 8.30am-7.30pm Mon-Sat; 🚇 Beyazıt-Kapalı Çarşı

Fashion designers and buyers from every corner of the globe know that this is where to come to source top-quality textiles in İstanbul. It's crammed with bolts of fabric, *pestemals* and scarves. Next-door Murat Danış is part of the same operation.

🍽 EAT

Generations of shoppers have worked up an appetite around the Grand Bazaar, and fortunately there have always been eateries to meet this need. These days, Western-style places such as Fes Cafe vie with traditional eateries

such as Havuzlu to keep tourists and locals well fed at lunchtime. Further down the hill near the Spice Bazaar are two kebap restaurants – Hamdi and Zinhan – that have magnificent views and are wonderful dinner destinations.

🍽 BAB-I HAYAT
Anatolian, Kebaps & Pides $$

Map p51; ☎ 212-520 7878; Mısır Çarşısı 47 (Spice Bazaar), Eminönü; ⏲ 11am-7pm Mon-Sat; 🚇 Eminönü

It took seven months for a team headed by one of the conservation architects from Topkapı Palace to restore and decorate this vaulted space over the eastern entrance to the Spice Bazaar. The result is an atmospheric setting in which to enjoy well-priced, unadorned Anatolian dishes. Enter through the Serhadoğlu fast-food shop.

🍽 FES CAFE *International* $

Map p53; ☎ 212-527 3684; Halıcılar Caddesi 62, Grand Bazaar; ⏲ 8.30am-7.30pm Mon-Sat; 🚇 Beyazıt-Kapalı Çarşı

Set in a rough-stone den, the popular Fes is one of the few Western-style cafes located in the Grand Bazaar. The flower-adorned tables are perfect spots to people-watch while having a drink and a bite to eat (sandwiches are the speciality and the coffee is excellent).

As Italy is to pizza, Turkey is to kebaps

🍴 HAFIZ MUSTAFA ŞEKERLEMELERİ
Sweets, Börek $

Map p51; ☎ 212-526 5627; Hamidiye Caddesi 84-86, Eminönü; 🕑 7.30am-11pm; 🚊 Eminönü

Choosing between the delicious baklava, tasty börek (filled savoury pastry) or indulgent *meshur tekirdağ peynir helvası* (a cheese-based sweet prepared with sesame oil, cereals and honey or syrup) is the challenge that confronts customers at this popular place. You can enjoy your choice with a glass of tea in the upstairs cafe.

🍴 HAMDİ ET LOKANTASI
Kebaps $$

Map p51; Hamdi Meat Restaurant; ☎ 212-528 0390; www.hamdirestorant .com.tr; Kalçın Sokak 17, Eminönü; 🕑 noon-11pm; 🚊 Eminönü

A favourite İstanbullu haunt since 1970, Hamdi's phenomenal views over the Golden Horne are matched by great food, professional service and a bustling atmosphere. Book online as far ahead of your meal as possible and request a spot on the terrace.

🍴 HAVUZLU RESTAURANT
Anatolian, Kebaps $$

Map p53; ☎ 212-527 3346; Gani Çelebi Sokak 3, Grand Bazaar; 🕑 11.30am-5pm Mon-Sat; 🚊 Beyazıt-Kapalı Çarşı

A lovely space with a vaulted ceiling, pale lemon walls and an ornate central light fitting, Havuzlu serves up good-quality *lokanta* (eatery serving ready-made food) fare (see p84) to hungry hordes of tourists and shopkeepers alike. It also has a clean toilet, something quite rare in the bazaar.

🍴 İMREN LOKANTASI
Anatolian, Kebabs $

Map p51; ☎ 212-638 1196; Kadırga Meydanı 143, Kadırga; ⏲ 7am-10.30pm; 🚇 Çemberlitaş

A tiny neighbourhood *lokanta* with extremely friendly staff, İmren is off the tourist trail but is worth the walk. It serves excellent, dirt-cheap dishes such as peppery lamb *guveç* (stew) or *musakka* (baked eggplant and minced meat). Go for lunch rather than dinner.

🍴 NAMLI *Delicatessen* $

Map p51; ☎ 212-511 6393; Hasırcılar Caddesi 14, Eminönü; ⏲ 7am-7pm Mon-Sat; 🚇 Eminönü

Namlı's mouth-watering selection of cheeses, *pastırma* (air-dried

beef) and meze are known throughout the city. Fight your way to the counter and order a tasty fried *pastırma* roll or a takeaway container of meze. In-the-know customers eat what they've bought upstairs in the cafeteria, where you can also grab a tasty light lunch. There's another branch in Karaköy (p86).

🍴 SUR OCAKBAŞI
Kebabs $$

Map p53; ☎ 212-533 8088; http://suro-cakbasi.net; İtfaiye Caddesi 27, Zeyrek; ⏲ 10am-11pm; 🚇 Aksaray

Tourists used to be a rare sight at this place nestled on a busy square in the shadow of the Aque-duct of Valens. But then Anthony

---

KEBAP KINGS

If Turkey has a signature dish, it has to be the kebap. Turks will tuck into anything cooked on a stick with gusto, and if asked where they would like to celebrate a special event, they will inevitably nominate one of the city's two most-famous *kebapçılar*: Develi and Beyti.

Develi (☎ 212-529 0833; www.develikebap.com; Gümüşyüzük Sokak 7, Samatya; mains TL14-30; ⏲ noon-midnight; 🚇 Koca Mustafa Paşa) opened its first restaurant in Kuruluş in 1912, but its most popular outlet is located at Samatya, in the shadow of Theodo-sius' Great Wall. The succulent kebaps here come in many guises and often reflect the season – the *keme kebabi* (truffle kebab) is only served for a few weeks each year, for instance. Prices are extremely reasonable for the quality of food that is on offer and the service is exemplary. Catch the train from Sirkeci or Cankurtaran.

Beyti (☎ 212-663 2990; www.beyti.com.tr; Orman Sokak 8, Florya; mains TL29-38; ⏲ noon-midnight Tue-Sun; 🚇 Florya) is located in an affluent suburb way out near Atatürk International Airport, but serious meat-lovers know that it's worth the trip. Mr Beyti's famous *kuzu şiş* (skewered lamb kebap) and other meat dishes are extraordinarily good and worth every *kuruş* (cent) of their relatively hefty price tags. Catch the train from Sirkeci or Cankurtaran.

Bourdain filmed a segment of *No Reservations* here and blew the place's cover. Come to enjoy the meat dishes and people-watching.

TARIHİ SÜLEYMANİYELİ FASÜLYECİ ERZİNCANLI ALI BABA *Anatolian* $

Map p51; ☎ 212-513 6219; Prof Sıddık Sami Onar Caddesi 11, Süleymaniye; ◷ 11am-4pm Mon-Sat; ℝ Beyazıt

Join the crowds of hungry locals at this institution in the former *kütüphanesi medrese* (theological-school library) of the Süleymaniye Mosque. It's been dishing up its spicy signature *fasülye* (broad bean) dish for more than 80 years. Try it with *ayran* (yoghurt drink).

ZEYREKHANE *Anatolian* $$

Map p51; ☎ 212-532 2778; İbadethane Arkası Sokak 10, Zeyrek; ◷ 9am-10pm Tue-Sun; ℝ Aksaray

This restaurant in the restored former *medrese* of Zeyrek Mosque (p56) also has an outdoor garden and terrace with magnificent views of the Golden Horn and back to the Süleymaniye Mosque. If the weather's good, it's a perfect spot for a simple lunch or sunset drink.

ZİNHAN KEBAP HOUSE AT STORKS

Kebaps, International $$

Map p51; ☎ 212-512 4275; www .zinhanrestaurant.com; Ragıpgümüşpala

Caddesi 2-5, Eminönü; ◷ noon-11pm; ℝ Eminönü

Zinhan's regal position next to the Galata Bridge is one of the best in the city. Its top-floor roof terrace offers sensational views and is an excellent place to enjoy a tasty kebap and salad meal served in elegant and extremely comfortable surrounds. Book ahead and request a table with a view.

DRINK

Coffee hit Turkey in the 10th century, but it wasn't until the mid-16th century that the first *kıraathaneler* (coffeehouses) were opened in İstanbul.

Unsurprisingly, they soon became a second home for İstanbullu males. These virtually private clubs were popular with specific clientele – one was for actors, another for mechanics, another for lawyers and so on. These days the *kıraathane* has been replaced by the simpler *kahveci* (coffeemaker). A handful of *kahveciler* still hold tight, particularly around the bazaar district.

ETHAM TEZÇAKAR KAHVECİ *Coffeehouse*

Map p53; Halıcılar Caddesi, Grand Bazaar; ◷ 8.30am-7.30pm Mon-Sat; ℝ Beyazıt-Kapalı Çarşı

This teeny coffee pit stop is smack bang in the middle of Halıcılar Caddesi. Its traditional brass-tray tables and wooden stools stand in stark contrast to the funky Fes Cafe (p63) opposite.

▼ FES CAFE *Cafe Bar*
Map p51; ☎ 212-526 3070; Alibaba Türbe Sokak 25-27, Nuruosmaniye; Closed Sun; **Ⓜ Beyazıt-Kapalı Çarşı**
After an afternoon spent trading repartee with the bazaar's touts, you'll be in need of a drink. Fortunately, this stylish cafe just outside the Nuruosmaniye Gate is a wonderful place to relax over a good-quality coffee, a beer or a glass of wine. It's also home to a branch of Abdulla Natural Products (p57).

BOZA
Worn out by the demands of too much sightseeing? *Boza* is your answer! This thick drink made from water, sugar and fermented bulgur has a reputation for building strength and virility. There's evidence that the Central Asian nomads of the 4th century AD enjoyed a version of *boza*, making it one of the oldest surviving Turkish foods. If you're staying in Sultanahmet you may hear the mobile *boza*-seller's melodious call as he walks the streets in winter. Otherwise, your best bet to try this rare treat is at Vefa Bozacısı (right).

▼ KAHVE DÜNYASI *Cafe*
Map p51; ☎ 212-527 3282; Nuruosmaniye Caddesi 79, Nuruosmaniye; 7.30am-9.30pm; **Ⓜ Çemberlitaş**
This branch of the popular 'coffee world' chain (see p89) is a comfortable spot for a caffeine fix and a bit of a sitdown.

▼ ŞARK KAHVESİ *Coffeehouse*
Map p53; ☎ 212-512 1144; Yağlıkçılar Caddesi 134, Grand Bazaar; 8.30am-7.30pm Mon-Sat; **Ⓜ Beyazıt-Kapalı Çarşı**
The Şark has long been the bazaar's best coffee stop. Travellers love the old photographs on the walls and the cheap tea and coffee.

▼ VEFA BOZACISI *Boza Bar*
Map p51; ☎ 212-519 4922; Katip Çelebi Caddesi 102, Vefa; 7am-midnight; **Ⓜ Beyazıt-Kapalı Çarşı**
İstanbul's most famous *boza* (see left) bar was established in 1876, and locals still flock to this location to imbibe. The viscous mucous-coloured beverage won't be to everyone's taste, but the bar – featuring blue tiles, marble tables and a glass that Atatürk drank out of in 1937 – is universally pleasing.

WORTH THE TRIP

İstanbul has more than its fair share of Byzantine monuments, but few are as drop-dead gorgeous as the **Chora Church** (Kariye Müsezi; ☎ 212-631 9241; Kariye Camii Sokak, Edirnekapı; admission TL15; 🕑 9am-6pm Thu-Tue Apr-Sep, to 4.30pm Oct-Mar). The fact that it's tucked away in the city's western districts means that many visitors overlook it. The exquisite mosaics and frescoes were commissioned by Theodore Metochites, the auditor of the imperial treasury, in 1312. Look out for the mosaic above the door to the nave in the inner narthex, which depicts Theodore offering the church to Christ.

Next door is the appetising **Asitane** (☎ 212-534 8414; www.asitanerestaurant.com; Kariye Camii Sokak 6, Edirnekapı; mains TL24-32; 🕑 11am-midnight), an elegant restaurant serving the most authentic Ottoman cuisine in town. The chefs here have tracked down recipes from the imperial kitchens of the Topkapı, Edirne and Dolmabahçe Palaces, which they prepare using original ingredients and cooking methods. Lunch is as delicious as it is unique.

While you're in the neighbourhood, don't forget to visit the **Mihrimah Sultan Mosque** (Ali Kuşçu Sokak, Edirnekapı), designed by Sinan and commissioned by Süleyman the Magnificent's favourite daughter, Mihrimah. The mosque occupies high ground right next to a section of the historic Theodosian Walls – the views of the defensive structure from this vantage point give a wonderful idea of what the walls must have looked like in their heyday.

To get here, catch bus 87 from Taksim Square or bus 31E, 32, 36KE or 37E from Eminönü.

⭐ PLAY

⭐ ERENLER AİLE ÇAY BAHÇESİ
Nargileh & Tea Garden
Map p51; Divan Yolu (Ordu) Caddesi 36, Çemberlitaş; 🕑 9am-midnight; 🚇 Beyazıt-Kapalı Çarşı
This nargileh place is located in the delightfully leafy courtyard of the Çorlulu Ali Paşa Camii Medrese. It's packed to the rafters with students from İstanbul University doing their best to live up to their genetic heritage and develop a life-long addiction to tobacco.

⭐ İLESAM LOKALI
Nargileh & Tea Garden
Map p51; Divan Yolu (Ordu) Caddesi 84, Çemberlitaş; 🕑 8am-midnight; 🚇 Çemberlitaş
This club in the courtyard of the Koca Sinan Paşa Medrese was formed by the enigmatically named Professional Union of Owners of the Works of Science & Literature. Fortunately, members seem happy for strangers to infiltrate their ranks. After entering the gate to Koca Sinan Paşa's tomb, go past the cemetery – it's the second teahouse to the right.

⭐ LALE BAHÇESİ
Nargileh & Tea Garden

Map p51; Şifahane Sokak, Süleymaniye; 🕑 9am-11pm; 🚇 Beyazıt-Kapalı Çarşı

In a sunken courtyard that was once part of the Süleymaniye *külliye*, this charming tea garden is always full of students from the nearby İstanbul University, who come here to spend a lazy hour or two on cushioned seats alongside a pretty fountain. In winter the students huddle inside the atmospheric kilim-clad *medrese*.

⭐ ŞAFAK SİNEMALARI *Cinema*

Map p51; ☎ 212-516 2660; Divan Yolu (Ordu) Caddesi 134, Çemberlitaş; tickets TL13; 🕑 9am-11pm; 🚇 Çemberlitaş

The only cinema close to Sultanahmet, the seven-screen Şafak Sinemaları screens mostly foreign films, though only of the wham-bam American blockbuster variety. Films are generally in English with Turkish subtitles, but double-check at the box office in case the film has Türkçe (Turkish) dubbing. Heavy petters sit up the back.

⭐ TÜRK OCAĞI KÜLTÜR VE SANAT MERKEZİ İKTİSADİ İŞLETMESİ ÇAY BAHÇESİ
Nargileh & Tea Garden

Map p51; cnr Divan Yolu (Ordu) & Babıalı Caddesis, Çemberlitaş; 🕑 8am-midnight, later in summer; 🚇 Çemberlitaş

Tucked into the rear right-hand corner of a shady Ottoman cemetery, this enormously popular tea garden is a perfect place to escape the crowds and relax over a tea and nargileh.

Spend an idle afternoon drinking tea and introducing yourself to nargileh (p138)

>BEYOĞLU & AROUND

The suburb of Beyoğlu (*bey*-oh-loo) rises from the shoreline north of the Golden Horn (Haliç) and incorporates the grand boulevard of İstiklal Caddesi (Independence Ave), known to locals simply as İstiklal. In the mid-19th century the suburb was known as Pera, and was home to the latest European fashions, patisseries, restaurants, boutiques and embassies.

BEYOĞLU & AROUND

Please see over for map

All this changed in the decades after the Republic was declared, when the embassies and their staff moved to Ankara. The glamorous shops and restaurants closed, the grand buildings crumbled and Beyoğlu took on a decidedly sleazy air. Fortunately the 1990s brought about a rebirth, and Beyoğlu is once again the heart of modern İstanbul, home to a huge range of shops, galleries, restaurants, bars and clubs. If you miss Beyoğlu, you haven't seen İstanbul.

To get to İstiklal Caddesi from Sultanahmet, take the tram. You can either get off at Karaköy and catch the Tünel (a funicular) to the western (bottom) end of İstiklal Caddesi, or you can get off at Kabataş, where the tram connects with a second funicular travelling up the hill to Taksim Square.

◉ SEE

Most sights are on or just off İstiklal Caddesi, which stretches from Tünel Square (C4) to Taksim Square (F1). An antique tram runs along its length, stopping at either end and at the Galatasaray Lycée along the way. In the late 19th century, İstiklal Caddesi was known as the Grande Rue de Pera, and the life of the modern city travelled up and down its lively promenade. Some things never change: come here between 4pm and 8pm daily – especially on Friday and Saturday – to see İstiklal at its busiest best. See also p16.

◎ AKBANK SANAT
☎ 212-252 3500; www.akbanksanat .com; cnr İstiklal Caddesi & Zambak Sokak; admission free; ⏰ 10.30am-7.30pm Tue-Sat; 🚇 Kabataş then funicular to Taksim Square
Turkey's big banks vie with each other to be seen as the greatest

sponsor of the arts. İstiklal is a showcase for their generosity, and with this venue Akbank joins Garanti and Yapı Kredi (see p77) in funding impressive exhibition spaces showcasing work by local and international artists.

◎ ÇİÇEK PASAJI
İstiklal Caddesi; ⏰ 9am-midnight; 🚇 Kabataş then funicular to Taksim Square
Back in the days when the *Orient Express* rolled into Old Stamboul, the Cité de Pera building was the most glamorous address in town. Built in 1876, it housed a shopping arcade as well as apartments. As Pera declined, so too did the building, with its stylish shops giving way to florists and then the *meyhaneler* (taverns; see p82 for more information) that are still operating today. We recommend walking through rather than eating here.

🎥 GALATA TOWER

Galata Kulesi; Galata Kulesi Meydanı, Galata; admission TL10; 🕙 **9am-8pm;** 🚊 **Karaköy then walk or funicular to Tünel**

Originally constructed in 1348, Galata Tower was the highest point in the Genoese fortifications of Galata. During the time of the Ottoman era it was mainly used as a lookout tower for the fires that regularly swept through the city. Though the view from the top is spectacular, we suggest enjoying it over a drink on the terrace of the Anemon Galata (p88) rather than paying the entry fee here.

🎥 GALERIST

☎ **212-244 8230; www.galerist.com .tr; 4th fl, İstiklal Caddesi 163, Galatasaray; admission free;** 🕙 **10am-6pm;** 🚊 **Karaköy then funicular to Tünel**

In the renovated Mısır Apartmentı building on İstiklal, this excellent commercial gallery shows work by some of the city's leading contemporary artists.

🎥 İSTANBUL MODERN

☎ **212-334 7300; www.istanbulmodern .org; Meclis-i Mebusan Caddesi, Tophane; adult/student/child under 12yr TL8/3/free, Thu free;** 🕙 **10am-6pm Tue, Wed & Fri-Sun, 10am-8pm Thu;** 🚊 **Tophane**

Galata Tower looms over the skyline like the tip of a giant pencil

WHIRLING INTO THE 21ST CENTURY

The brotherhood called the Mevlevi, or whirling dervishes, follow a mystical form of Islam, using allegorical language to describe a love for God. They are best known for their meditative *sema*, a whirling ceremony that represents a union with God.

The Mevlevi are guided by the teachings of Celaleddin Rumi, known as Mevlana (Our Guide). Born in 1207, Rumi was a brilliant student of Islamic theology who became profoundly influenced by Şemsi Tebrizi, a Sufi (Muslim mystic) disciple.

The Mevlevi order was outlawed by Atatürk in the 1920s as part of his reforms, but in the early 1950s the Turkish government recognised the tourist potential for 'whirling' and the Konya Mevlana Festival was born. The whirling dervish 'performance' is a growing drawcard for visitors to Turkey, but the Mevlevi order is still technically outlawed in the country.

See p49 for an opportunity to see the dervishes whirling when you're in town.

This is the big daddy of a slew of new, privately funded art galleries in the city. Its stunning location on the shore of the Bosphorus and its extensive collection of 20th-century Turkish art make it well worth a visit. Icing on the cake is provided by a constantly changing and uniformly excellent program of exhibitions by local and international artists in the temporary galleries on the ground floor. See also p17.

◉ MEVLEVİ MUSEUM

Galata Mevlevihanesi Müzesi, Divan Edebiyatı Müzesi; ☎ 212-245 4141; Galipdede Caddesi 15, Tünel; 🚇 Karaköy then funicular to Tünel
Most of the *tekkeler* (dervish lodges) in İstanbul are in ruins, but this one – parts of which date from 1491 – has survived and was undergoing a major renovation

when this book went to print. When it reopens it may host a weekly *sema* (whirling dervish ceremony). Check the board outside for details.

◉ PERA MUSEUM

☎ 212-334 9900; www.peramuzesi .org.tr; Meşrutiyet Caddesi 65, Tepebaşı; adult/student/child under 12yr TL7/3/ free; 🕙 10am-7pm Tue-Sat, noon-6pm Sun; 🚇 Karaköy then funicular to Tünel
If, like so many travellers, you've seen reproductions of the famous Osman Hamdı Bey painting *The Tortoise Trainer* and fallen in love with it, the Pera Museum is the place to view the real thing. It's part of the museum's wonderful collection of Orientalist paintings, which occupies the 3rd floor. Excellent temporary exhibitions of international contemporary art are held here, too. See also p17.

Refika Birgül
Chef and author of Refika's Kitchen: Cooking New Istanbul Style

What is distinctive about İstanbullu cuisine? It is strong and assured fusion food based on classic Turkish food roots and made with a mixture of *emek* (hard work) and heart. **Do you have favourite restaurants in the city?** There are many, but I particularly enjoy the food at Changa (p83), Çiya Sofrasi (p48) and Cercis Murat Konağı (☎ 216-373 1193; www.cercismurat .com, in Turkish; Yazmacı Tahir Sokak 22, Suadiye; mains TL25; 🕙 10am-midnight). **Are locals interested in food culture?** Very! I write a weekly full-page column in the nationwide *Hürriyet* newspaper where I discuss issues about food, and people are very interested. **You have been referred to as the local equivalent of Jamie Oliver. Do you admire him?** Of course! I want to promote cooking culture in Turkey as he does in the UK. And like him, I feel passionately about many things, for instance the death of neighbourhood shops at the hands of big supermarkets.

🄲 TAKSİM SQUARE

Taksim Meydanı; 🚇 Kabataş then funicular to Taksim Square

This square is named after the stone reservoir on its western side, but it's better known as the symbolic heart of the modern city. The prominent modern building on its eastern side is the Atatürk Cultural Centre, home to the city's ballet and opera companies. Designed by Hayati Tabanlıoğlu in 1956–57, it appears to best advantage at night when its elegant steel mesh is illuminated.

🄲 YAPI KREDİ CULTURAL CENTRE

☎ 212-252 4700; www.ykykultur.com.tr; İstiklal Caddesi 161, Galatasaray; admission free; 🕙 10am-7pm Mon-Fri, 10am-6pm Sat, 1-6pm Sun; 🚇 Karaköy, then funicular to Tünel

This centre features a exhibition program including everything from retrospectives of 20th-century Turkish painters to spotlights on contemporary photographers working in İstanbul. It's funded by the Yapı Kredi bank, which has a history of funding Turkish art.

🏃 DO

🄲 YEŞİLDİREK HAMAMI
Gay Hamam

☎ 212-297 7223; Tersane Caddesi 74, Azapkapı; bath TL20, with massage TL30; 🕙 6am-9pm; 🚇 Karaköy

This spacious, well-maintained *hamam* (bathhouse) is located at the base of the Atatürk Bridge and has all the traditional trappings. It's crowded with testosterone-laden bathhouse-lovers, including expats and in-the-know tourists. Be discreet.

🄲 SHOP

İstiklal Caddesi has a long history as the city's most glamorous shopping strip but has lost its sheen in recent years, probably due to the phenomenal popularity of the glam shopping malls opening in the affluent suburbs north of Beyoğlu (see the boxed text, p100). You'll find the city's best book and music shops here, but not much else worthy of comment.

Next to Çiçek Pasajı (p71), along Sahne Sokak (D2), is Beyoğlu's Balık Pazar (Fish Market), with stalls selling fruit, vegetables, caviar, pickles and other produce. Leading off the Balık Pazar is the neoclassical Avrupa Pasajı (D2), a pretty passageway with a handful of shops selling tourist wares and antique prints. Aslıhan Pasajı (D2), nearby, is a two-storey arcade bursting with second-hand books. Around the Tünel end of İstiklal, you'll find musical instrument shops on the walk down Galipdede Caddesi (C4–C5) to Galata Tower.

Antique stores can be found dotting the narrow winding streets of Çukurcuma and stylish fashion boutiques are found on Serder-ı Ekrem Caddesi in Galata, in trendy Şişhane and in the expat enclave of Cihangir.

◙ ALİ MUHİDDİN HACI BEKİR
Food & Drink
☎ 212-245 1375; İstiklal Caddesi 83; 🚇 Kabataş then funicular to Taksim Square
This is the Beyoğlu branch of the famous *lokum* (Turkish delight) shop (p57).

◙ ARTRIUM
Antiques & Ceramics, Prints
☎ 212-251 4302; Tünel Geçidi 7, Tünel; 🚇 Karaköy then funicular to Tünel
One of the original shops in this hip precinct, Artrium stocks antique ceramics, miniatures, maps, prints and jewellery. There's something for everyone here, ranging from superb items for serious collectors to a great range of Ottoman etchings for people wanting to buy a little something for the lounge room back home.

◙ DOORS *Clothing*
☎ 212-245 7886; Ensiz Sokak 1B, Tünel; 🕙 9am-8pm Mon-Sat & noon-6pm Sun; 🚇 Karaköy then funicular to Tünel
Local fashion designer Ümit Ünal designs women's clothes that

are best described as wearable art – they're rapidly developing an international following.

◙ ELVIS *Musical Instruments*
☎ 212-293 8752; Galipdede Caddesi 35, Tünel; 🕙 10am-6pm; 🚇 Karaköy then funicular to Tünel
If you thought Elvis was hiding in the Bahamas, you're wrong. He's here, selling a good range of traditional stringed instruments.

◙ HİKMET + PINAR
Antiques
☎ 212-293 0575; Faik Paşa Yokuşu 36A, Çukurcuma; 🕙 10am-6pm; 🚇 Kabataş then funicular to Taksim Square
Quality always comes at a price, so you should only enter this opulent antiques store if you're able to spend the cash equivalent of a second mortgage. It'll be fun, though!

◙ HOMER KİTABEVİ *Books*
☎ 212-249 5902; www.homerbooks .com; Yeni Çarşı Caddesi 12, Galatasaray; 🕙 10am-7.30pm Mon-Sat, 12.30-7.30pm Sun; 🚇 Kabataş then funicular to Taksim Square
Come here for an unrivalled range of Turkish fiction, plus an enviable collection of nonfiction covering everything from Sufism and Islam to Kurdish and Armenian issues. It stocks children's books too.

📷 İSTANBUL KİTAPÇISI
Books & Music, Maps & Prints
☎ 212-292 7692; www.istanbulkitap
cisi.com; İstiklal Caddesi 379; 🕑 10am-
6.45pm Mon-Sat, noon-6.45pm Sun;
🚇 Karaköy then funicular to Tünel
This government-run bookshop
has English-language books on
İstanbul, a wide-ranging selection of maps and music, and the
cheapest prints you'll find any-
where in the city.

📷 İSTANBUL MODERN GIFT
SHOP *Gifts, Souvenirs*
☎ 212-334 7300; www.istanbul
modern.org; Meclis-i Mebusan Caddesi,
Tophane; 🕑 10am-6pm Tue, Wed
& Fri-Sun, 10am-8pm Thu; 🚇 Tophane
It's often difficult to source
well-priced souvenirs and gifts to
take home, but this stylish shop
in the İstanbul Modern gallery
sells suitable items aplenty. The
cute gifts for kids are particularly
noteworthy, and there's also a
good selection of jewellery and
stationery.

📷 LALE PLAK
Music
☎ 212-293 7739; Galipdede Caddesi 1,
Tünel; 🕑 9am-7.30pm Mon-Sat,
11.30am-7pm Sun; 🚇 Karaköy then
funicular to Tünel
This long-standing magnet for
music aficionados is crammed
with Turkish music and jazz CDs.

📷 LEYLA SEYHANLI
Clothing
☎ 212-293 7410; Altıpatlar Sokak
20, Çukurcuma; 🕑 11am-5.30pm;
🚇 Kabataş then funicular to Taksim
Square
If you love old clothes, you'll adore
Leyla Seyhanlı's boutique. Filled
to the brim with piles of Ottoman
embroidery and outfits, it's a rum-
mager's delight.

📷 MARIPOSA *Clothing*
☎ 212-249 0483; Şimşirci Sokak 11A,
Cihangir; 🕑 10am-8.30pm Mon-Fri,
11am-8.30pm Sat & Sun; 🚇 Kabataş
then funicular to Taksim Square
The Mariposa atelier turns out a
particularly fetching line of floral
frocks. Those devoted to fashion
will adore the fact that it not only
makes to order, but also designs
and tailors unique ensembles.
As well as the dresses, coats and
jackets on the racks, Mariposa
makes pretty bedspreads and
pillowslips.

📷 MEPHISTO *Music*
☎ 212-249 0687; www.mephisto
.com.tr; İstiklal Caddesi 125; 🕑 9am-
midnight; 🚇 Kabataş then funicular to
Taksim Square
If you develop a taste for Turkish
music while you're in town, this
is the place to indulge it. It has a
large range of pop, rap, hip-hop
and electronica.

☐ PANDORA *Books*

☎ 212-243 3503; Büyükparmakkapı Sokak 8B; ☾ 10am-8pm Mon-Wed, 10am-9pm Thu-Sat & 1-8pm Sun; 🚇 Kabataş then funicular to Taksim Square

This long-standing independent bookshop has recently opened a new store dedicated solely to English-language books. It has great crime fiction and travel sections, as well as loads of books about Turkey.

☐ PAŞABAHÇE *Glassware*

☎ 212-244 0544, İstiklal Caddesi 314; ☾ 10am-8pm Mon-Sat, 11am-7pm Sun; 🚇 Karaköy then funicular to Tünel

First established on the Bosphorus in 1957, Paşabahçe has gone from strength to strength. It exports its glassware internationally, but the three-storey emporium is the best place to get both the latest fashion glassware pieces and stock-standard items. There's another branch on Teşvikiye Caddesi in Nişantaşı (p97).

☐ ROBINSON CRUSOE *Books*

☎ 212-293 6968; İstiklal Caddesi 389; ☾ 9am-9.30pm Mon-Sat, 10am-9.30pm Sun; 🚇 Karaköy then funicular to Tünel

We can think of few more pleasant fates than being stranded here for a couple of hours. It stocks a wide range of English-language novels and magazines, as well as a good range of books about İstanbul.

Browse Robinson Crusoe's top shelf – if you dare

☐ SIR *Ceramics*

☎ 212-293 3661; www.sircini.com; Serdar-ı Ekrem Sokak 38, Galata; ☾ 11am-7pm Mon-Sat; 🚇 Karaköy then walk or funicular to Tünel

Ceramics produced in İstanbul can be prohibitively pricey, but the attractive hand-painted plates, platters, bowls and tiles sold at this small atelier are exceptions to the rule.

🍴 EAT

Beyoğlu is where you should come to eat, drink and be merry. *Meyhane* strips such as Nevizade and Sofyalı Sokaks (D2 and C4) are busy every night of the week, and the streets off İstiklal Caddesi are filled with eateries catering to every palate and budget. To savour the top-notch cuisine served at glam establishments such as Mikla (p86) and Changa (p83) you'll need to book ahead, but you'll be able to walk into many others and score a table. Down in Galata and Karaköy there are a few long-standing favourites and one or two up-and-comers – it's busier during the day here than it is at night.

🍴 9 ECE AKSOY
Anatolian $$$

☎ 212-245 7628; www.dokuzeceaksoy .com; Otelier Sokak 9, Tepebaşı; ⏱ noon-midnight; 🚡 Karaköy then funicular to Tünel

The cool jazz on the soundtrack suits the warm-toned casual interior of this modern *meyhane* near the Pera Palace Hotel. The lady chef/host here is a true believer in the superiority of local and organic produce, which she uses to make her flavoursome dishes. Don't miss the mezes.

🍴 ANTİOCHİA *Anatolian* $$

☎ 212-292 1100; www.antiochia concept.com; Minare Sokak 21, Asmalımescit; ⏱ closed Sun; 🚡 Karaköy then funicular to Tünel

Dishes from the southeastern city of Antakya (Hatay) are the speciality of this recently opened restaurant in Asmalımescit. Sit inside or in the quiet pedestrianised street to sample meze plates featuring salads dominated by wild thyme, pomegranate syrup, olives, walnuts, hot pepper and tangy home-made yoghurt. The choice of kebaps is equally unusual and delicious. Yum.

🍴 BIG CHEFS
International $$

☎ 212-251 7180; www.bigchefs.com .tr; Meşrutiyet Caddesi 176, Şişhane; ⏱ 8am-midnight; 🚡 Karaköy then funicular to Tünel

Şişhane is the hottest neighbourhood in the city right now, and Big Chefs is one of the reasons why. A modern space that wouldn't be out of place in New York or London, it offers a suitably international menu featuring sandwiches, wraps, burgers, salads, pastas, pizzas and a few kebaps.

🍴 BONCUK RESTAURANT
Anatolian, Fish $$

☎ 212-243 1219; Nevizade Sokak 19; ⏱ 11am-1am; 🚡 Kabataş then funicular to Taksim Square

Armenian specialities differentiate Boncuk from its Nevizade Sokak neighbours. Try the excellent, super-fresh *topik* (meze made from chickpeas, pistachios, onion, flour, currants, cumin and salt). Arrive early and book ahead to get a table on the street, which is where all the action occurs.

🍴 CANIM CİĞERİM İLHAN USTA *Anatolian* $

☎ 212-252 6060; Minare Sokak 1, Asmalımescit; 🕙 10am-midnight; 🚇 Karaköy then funicular to Tünel

The name means 'my soul, my liver', and this small place behind the Ali Hoca Türbesi specialises in a set meal (TL11 to TL18) of grilled liver served with herbs, *ezme* (spicy tomato sauce) and grilled vegetables. If you can't bring yourself to eat offal, fear not – you can choose to substitute liver with lamb or chicken. No alcohol.

🍴 CEZAYIR
Modern Mediterranean $$

☎ 212-245 9980; www.cezayir-istanbul .com; Hayriye Caddesi 16, Galatasaray; 🕙 noon-11.30pm; 🚇 Kabataş then funicular to Taksim Square

Housed in an attractive building that was once home to an Italian school, Cezayir is heavy on charm and relatively light on the wallet. The food is Mod Med with Turkish influences and the crowd is upmarket boho. In summer, the courtyard is always packed with happy diners.

MEYHANELER – THE BIGGEST PARTY IN TOWN

If you only have one night out on the town when you're in İstanbul, make sure you spend it at a *meyhane* (tavern). On every night of the week, *meyhaneler* such as Karaköy Lokantası (p84) and Sofyalı 9 (p86) are full of groups of chattering locals choosing from the dizzying array of meze and fish dishes on offer, washed down with a never-ending supply of rakı (aniseed brandy). On Friday and Saturday nights, *meyhane* precincts such as Nevizade and Sofyalı Sokaks literally heave with people and are enormously enjoyable places to be.

Traditional *meyhaneler* often host musicians playing *fasıl*, a lively local form of Gypsy music. The best of these is **Despina** (☎ 212-247 3357; Açıkyol Sokak 9, Kurtuluş; dinner incl drinks TL50; 🕙 noon-12.30am Mon-Sat, music 8.30pm-midnight most nights), which was established in 1946 and is known for its excellent music. It's way off the well-beaten tourist track and is hard to find – ask your hotel to organise a taxi. Other options include **Cumhuriyet** (☎ 212-293 1977; Sahne Sokak 4; set menus TL55-65; 🕙 9am-2am, music 8.30pm-midnight most nights; 🚇 Kabataş then funicular to Taksim Square) in Beyoğlu's Balık Pazar (Fish Market), and **Demeti** (🕙 212-244 0628; Şimşirci Sokak 6, Cihangir; set menus TL55-65; 🕙 closed Sun; 🚇 Kabataş then funicular to Taksim Square).

If you eat at a *meyhane* where there's live music, make sure you tip the musicians when they play at your table, as they work for tips rather than salary. Between TL5 to TL10 for each person at the table is about right.

🍴 CHANGA
Modern International $$$

☎ 212-249 1348; www.changa-istanbul
.com; Sıraselviler Caddesi 47, Taksim;
⏱ 6pm-1am Mon-Sat Nov-May;
🚇 Kabataş then funicular to Taksim Square

Lots of eateries in İstanbul attempt fusion cuisine, but few do it well. Peter Gordon, executive chef at this glamorous restaurant, is one who does. Dishes such as his roasted salmon with miso and coconut sauce served with a coriander and rose-petal salad are simply spectacular. In summer, the action moves to Müzedechanga (p117) on the Bosphorus.

🍴 DOĞA BALIK
Anatolian, Fish $$

☎ 212-293 9144; www.dogabalik.com; 7th fl, Villa Zurich Hotel, Akarsu Yokuşu Caddesi 36, Cihangir; ⏱ noon-11pm; 🚇 Kabataş then funicular to Taksim Square

There's something fishy about this place – and the locals love it. On the top floor of a hotel in Cihangir, Doğa Balık serves fabulously fresh fish in a dining space with wonderful views across to the Old City. It also has a lavish meze buffet.

🍴 FASULI LOKANTALARI
Anatolian $

☎ 212-243 6580; www.fasuli.com.tr; İskele Caddesi 10-12, Tophane; ⏱ 7am-11pm; 🚇 Tophane

There are two types of *fasulye* (broad bean) dishes served in Turkey: Anatolian-style Erzincan beans cooked in a spicy tomato sauce; and Black Sea–style beans cooked in a red gravy full of butter and meat. This *lokanta* (eatery serving ready-made food) next to the nargileh (water pipe) joints in Tophane serves its delicious beans Black Sea style, and also serves other specialties from the region, including *mihlama* (Turkish fondue made with corn, butter and cheese).

🍴 HACI ABDULLAH
Anatolian, Ottoman $$

☎ 212-293 8561; www.haciabdullah .com.tr; Sakızağacı Caddesi 9A; ⏱ 11am-11pm; 🚇 Kabataş then funicular to Taksim Square

Just thinking about Hacı Abdullah's sensational *imam bayıldı* (eggplant stuffed with tomatoes, onions and garlic and slow cooked in olive oil) makes our tastebuds go into overdrive. This İstanbul institution (it was established in 1888) is one of the city's best *lokantas* (see the boxed text, p84), and is one of the essential gastronomic stops you should make when in town. No alcohol is served.

🍴 KAFE ARA
International $$

☎ 212-245 4104; Tosbağ Sokak 8A; ⏱ 8am-midnight; 🚇 Kabataş then funicular to Taksim Square

In the Beyoğlu popularity stakes this cafe stands head and shoulders above the rest. A funky converted garage with tables and chairs spilling out into a wide laneway opposite the Galatasaray Lycée, it's a casual and welcoming setting in which to enjoy well-priced paninis, salads and pastas. No alcohol.

🍴 KAHVEDAN
International $

☎ 212-292 4030; Akarsu Yokuşu Caddesi 50, Cihangir; ◷ 9am-2am Mon-Fri, to 4am Sat & Sun; 🚇 Kabataş then funicular to Taksim Square

This expatriate haven serves dishes such as bacon and eggs, French toast, *mee goreng* and falafel wraps. Owner Shellie Corman is a traveller at heart, and knows how important things such as free wi-fi, decent wine by the glass, keen prices and good music are.

🍴 KARAKÖY GÜLLÜOĞLU
Baklava, Börek $

☎ 212-293 0910; Rıhtım Caddesi, Katlı Otopark Altı, Karaköy; ◷ 8am-7pm Mon-Sat; 🚇 Karaköy

The Güllü family opened its first baklava shop in Karaköy in 1949, and it's been making customers deliriously happy and dentists obscenely rich ever since. Go to the register and pay for a glass of tea and a *porsiyon* (portion) of whatever baklava takes your fancy (*fıstıklı* is pistachio, *cevizli* is walnut and *sade* is plain). You then queue to receive a plate with two or three pieces, depending on the type you order. The börek (filled savoury pastry) here is also exceptionally fine.

🍴 KARAKÖY LOKANTASI
Anatolian $$

☎ 212-292 4455; Kemankeş Caddesi 37, Karaköy; ◷ noon-4pm & 6pm-midnight Mon-Sat; 🚇 Karaköy

LOVIN' THOSE LOKANTAS

If the Turkish heart lies with the *meyhane*, its stomach rests with the *lokanta*. Serving *hazır yemek* (ready-made food) kept warm in bain-maries, these places are where the locals come for belly fuel at lunchtime. You'll find every type in town, from no-nonsense workers' places serving what can only be described as stodge to elegant establishments offering some of the best food you'll ever sample. The etiquette is the same at all: check out what's in the bain-marie and tell the waiter or cook behind the counter what you would like to eat. You can order a full *porsiyon* (portion), a half *(yarım) porsiyon* or a plate with a few choices – you'll be charged by the portion. After taking a seat, you'll then be served your chosen plate of food by a waiter.

The city's best *lokantas* include Çiya Sofrası in Kadıköy (see the boxed text, p48), Hacı Abdullah (p83), Karaköy Lokantası (p84) and Hünkar (p98).

This family-run *lokanta* opposite the International Maritime Passenger Terminal has a gorgeous tiled interior that was designed by the wildly fashionable Autoban Design Partnership. The dishes here are tasty and well priced, and service is both friendly and efficient. The place functions as a *lokanta* during the day, but at night it morphs into a popular *meyhane,* with slightly higher prices and some streetside tables. If you're here for lunch, consider skipping dessert and decamping to nearby Karaköy Güllüoğlu to sample its deservedly famous baklava.

KONAK

Anatolian, Kebaps & Pide　　　$

☎ 212-252 0684; İstiklal Caddesi 259, Galatasaray; ⏲ 7.30am-11.30pm; 🚋 Kabataş then funicular to Taksim Square

Eateries on İstiklal are often dreadful, but this long-time favourite place bucks the trend. It serves excellent kebaps and pides; try the delectable İskender kebap and follow this up with a serving of Turkey's famous but hard-to-find Maraş ice cream and we promise you'll be both happy and replete. There is also another branch near Tünel, but this one is much better.

Taking the order at Kafe Ara (p83)

🍴 MEDİ ŞARK SOFRASI
Kebaps $$

☎ 212-244 9056; Küçük Parmak Kapı Sokak 46a; ⏱ 11.30am-midnight; 🚇 Kabataş then funicular to Taksim Square

This excellent *kebapcı* specialises in meat dishes from the southeastern region of Turkey, served with the house speciality of *babam ekmek* ('my father's bread'). Everyone loves the frothy home-made *ayran* (yoghurt drink). No alcohol is served.

🍴 MİKLA
Modern Mediterranean $$$

☎ 0212-293 5656; www.mikla restaurant.com; Marmara Pera Hotel, Meşrutiyet Caddesi 15, Tepebaşı; ⏱ 6.30-11.30pm Mon-Sat; 🚇 Karaköy then funicular to Tünel

Local celebrity chef Mehmet Gürs serves the best Mediterranean cuisine in the city, and the Turkish accents he employs make his food memorable. Mikla is his flagship restaurant and it has retained its glamour tag for years – no mean achievement in this town of fleeting trends and fickle fashionistas. The views here are extraordinary (ask for a table with a view of the Old City) and the surrounds luxurious. Sadly, service can be grudging.

🍴 NAMLI *Delicatessen* $

☎ 212-293 6880; Rıhtım Caddesi, Karaköy; ⏱ 7am-10pm; 🚇 Karaköy

The Karaköy branch of the city's best delicatessen (p65).

🍴 SARAY MUHALLEBİCİSİ
Sweets $

☎ 212-292 3434; İstiklal Caddesi 173; ⏱ 6am-2am; 🚇 Kabataş then funicular to Taksim Square

This *muhallebici* (milk-pudding shop) is owned by İstanbul's mayor, no less. It's been dishing up puddings since 1935 and is packed with locals scratching their heads over which of the 35-odd varieties of sweets they want to try this time. Try the *fırın sütlaç* (rice pudding), *aşure* (dried fruit, nut and pulse pudding) or *kazandibi* (slightly burnt chicken-breast pudding).

🍴 SOFYALI 9 *Anatolian, Fish* $$

☎ 212-245 0362; Sofyalı Sokak 9, Tünel; ⏱ 11am-1am Mon-Sat; 🚇 Karaköy then funicular to Tünel

Tables here are hot property on Friday and Saturday night, and no wonder. This gem of a place serves up some of the city's best *meyhane* food, and does so in surroundings as welcoming as they are attractive. Regulars swear by the *Arnavut ciğeri* (Albanian fried liver), fried fish and exceptionally fine meze.

🍴 TARİHİ KARAKÖY BALIK LOKANTASI *Fish* $$

☎ 212-251 1371; Kardeşim Sokak 30, off Yüzbaşı Sabahattin Evren Caddesi,

Karaköy; 🕐 11.30am-3.30pm Mon-Sat;
🚋 Karaköy

Walk through the rundown quarter behind the Karaköy Fish Market and you'll come across this unassuming treasure, one of the few old-style fish restaurants remaining on the Golden Horn. Everything is so fresh it's almost writhing – the fish baked in paper is a taste sensation and the dirt-cheap fish soup is the best in town. No alcohol.

🍴 ZENCEFİL
Organic, Vegetarian $

☎ 212-243 8234; Kurabiye Sokak 8;
🕐 11am-11pm Mon-Sat; 🚋 Kabataş
then funicular to Taksim Square

This popular vegetarian cafe is comfortable and quietly stylish. Try the daily and weekly specials to get crunchy-fresh produce (all organic) and guilt-free desserts. The slabs of homemade bread are a definite highlight.

🍴 ZÜBEYIR OCAKBAŞI
Anatolian $$

☎ 212-293 3951; Bekar Sokak 28;
🕐 noon-midnight; 🚋 Kabataş then
funicular to Taksim Square

Every morning, the chefs at this popular *ocakbaşı* (barbecue restaurant) prepare the fresh, top-quality meats that will be grilled over their handsome copper-hooded barbeques that night: spicy chicken wings and Adana kebaps, flavour-

some ribs, pungent liver kebaps, and well-marinated lamb *şiş kebaps*. Their succulent offerings are known throughout the city, so booking a table is essential. Sit inside next to the grill, or on the streetside tables.

🍸 DRINK

There are hundreds of bars in Beyoğlu. The most popular bar precincts are on or around Balo Sokak (D2) and Sofyalı Sokak (C4), but there are also a number of sleek bars on roof terraces on both sides of İstiklal – these have views and prices to match. Strangely, decent coffee is hard to come by.

🍸 5 KAT *Bar*

☎ 212-293 3774; www.5kat.com; 5th fl,
Soğancı Sokak 7, Cihangir; 🕐 10am-
1.30am; 🚋 Kabataş then funicular to
Taksim Square

This İstanbul institution is a great alternative for those who can't stomach the style overload at 360 and the like. In winter, drinks are served in the boudoir-style bar; in summer, action moves to the outdoor terrace. Both have great Bosphorus views.

🍸 360 *Bar*

☎ 212-251 1042; www.360istanbul
.com; 8th fl, Mısır Apartmentı, İstiklal
Caddesi 311, Galatasaray; 🕐 noon-2am
Mon-Thu & Sun, 3pm-4am Fri & Sat;
🚋 Karaköy then funicular to Tünel

İstanbul's most famous bar, and deservedly so. If you can score one of the bar stools on the terrace you'll be happy indeed – the view is truly extraordinary. It morphs into a club after midnight on Fridays and Saturdays. Note: food here can be disappointing.

☙ ANEMON GALATA
Hotel Bar

☎ 212-293 2343; Galata Kulesi Meydanı, Galata; ✆ 6pm-midnight; 🚇 Karaköy then walk or funicular to Tünel

This eyrie on top of a restored Ottoman hotel is one of the best places in the city to watch the sunset while contemplating a cocktail. Views over to Galata Tower, the Old City and across the Golden Horn are stunning.

☙ BADEHANE *Bar*

☎ 212-249 0550; General Yazgan Sokak 5, Tünel; ✆ 9am-2am; 🚇 Karaköy then funicular to Tünel

This tiny unsigned watering hole is a favourite with locals because of its cheap beer. On a balmy evening the laneway is crammed with chattering, chain-smoking artsy types sipping a beer or three;

Relax over a drink and enjoy wonderful views at Leb-İ-Derya (p89)

when it's cold they squeeze inside. Dress down and come ready to enjoy an attitude-free evening.

☿ CLUB 17
Gay Bar

Zambak Sokak 17; cover incl 1 drink TL10 (Fri & Sat only); ☾ **11pm-4am Sun-Thu, 11pm-5.30am Fri & Sat;** ☖ **Kabataş then funicular to Taksim Square**

Techno music and a jam-packed interior are the hallmarks of this gay bar. At closing time, there's a veritable meat rack outside.

☿ KAHVE DÜNYASI
Cafe

☎ **212-293 1206; Meclis-i Mebusan Caddesi, Tütün Han 167, Tophane;** ☾ **7.30am-9.30pm;** ☖ **Tophane**

The name means 'coffee world', and this new coffee chain has the local world at its feet. The secret of its success lies with its huge coffee menu, reasonable prices, delicious chocolate spoons (yes, you read that correctly), comfortable seating and free wi-fi. The filter coffee is better than its espresso-based alternatives. You'll find other branches throughout the city, including one in the bazaar district (p67).

☿ LEB-İ DERYA *Bar*

☎ **212-293 4989; www.lebiderya.com; 6th fl, Kumbaracı Yokuşu 57, Tünel;** ☾ **4pm-2am Mon-Thu, 4pm-3am Fri,**

10am-3am Sat, 10am-2am Sun; ☖ **Karaköy then funicular to Tünel**

Ask many İstanbullus to name their favourite watering hole and they're likely to nominate this unpretentious place. On the top floor of a dishevelled building off Istiklal, it has wonderful views across to the Old City and down the Bosphorus, meaning that seats on the small outdoor terrace or at the bar are highly prized.

☿ LEB-İ DERYA RICHMOND
Bar

☎ **212-243 4375; www.lebiderya.com; 6th fl, Richmond Hotel, İstiklal Caddesi 227, Tünel;** ☾ **11am-2am Mon-Thu, 11am-3am Fri, 10am-3pm Sat, 10am-2am Sun;** ☖ **Karaköy then funicular to Tünel**

This sleek older sister to the original Leb-i Derya is more restrained and decidedly more chic than her little sis. Fortunately there's no threat of sibling rivalry – the crowd here is older and more cashed-up. The views from the huge windows are just as fab.

☿ MAVRA *Bar/Cafe*

☎ **212-252 7488; Serdar-ı Ekrem Caddesi 31A, Galata;** ☾ **9am-2am Mon-Fri, 9am-4pm Sat & Sun;** ☖ **Karaköy then funicular to Tünel**

Serdar-ı Ekrem Caddesi is one of Galata's most interesting streets, full of ornate 19th-century apartment blocks and avant-garde boutiques. During the day this popular place functions as a cafe; at night it reinvents itself as a hip bar.

Y MİKLA Bar
☎ 0212-293 5656; www.mikla restaurant.com; Marmara Pera Hotel, Meşrutiyet Caddesi 15, Tepebaşı; 🕙 from 6.30pm Mon-Sat summer only; 🚇 Karaköy then funicular to Tünel
It's worth overlooking the occasionally uppity service at this stylish rooftop bar to enjoy what could well be the best view in İstanbul. After a couple of drinks, move downstairs to the sophisticated restaurant (p86) so that you can sample some of its Mod Med cuisine. Quintessentially İstanbul.

Y OTTO Bar/Café
☎ 212-252 6588; www.ottoistanbul .com; Sofyalı Sokak 22, Tünel; 🕙 11am-2am; 🚇 Karaköy then funicular to Tünel
At the hub of the Sofyalı party precinct, Otto is a perfect place for a drink before dinner at one of the Asmalımescit restaurants.

Y PUBLIC Bar, Club
☎ 212-251 5131; Meşrutiyet Caddesi 84, Şişhane; 🕙 9am-midnight, to 4am Thu-Sat; 🚇 Karaköy then funicular to Tünel
The best thing to occur in Şişhane since the metro station opened, this stylish bar/restaurant/nightclub is popular with the city's

Bebek-based glamour gurus, who all flock here to party on weekends.

Y WHITE MILL Bar, Cafe
☎ 212-292 2895; www.whitemillcafe .com; Susam Sokak 13, Cihangir; 🕙 9.30am-1.30am; 🚇 Kabataş then funicular to Taksim Square
A favourite with the expats and arty İstanbullus who call Cihangir home, White Mill's couch-filled interior and fabulous rear garden are inevitably full of 20-somethings enjoying great music and a decidedly hip ambience. Its kitchen specialises in simple comfort foods.

Y X BAR Bar
☎ 212-244 7101; www.xrestaurantbar .com; 7th fl, Sadı Konuralp Caddesi 5, Şişhane; 🕙 noon-midnight; 🚇 Karaköy then funicular to Tünel
High culture meets serious glamour at this bar-restaurant on the top floor of the İstanbul Foundation for Culture and Arts (İKS––V) building in artsy Şişhane. Come here for a sunset aperitif or two – the Golden Horn view is simply extraordinary.

⭐ PLAY
Although the best clubbing action is down on the Bosphorus, Beyoğlu still reigns supreme when it comes to live music. If you're after

Grab a drink at 360, İstanbul's most famous bar (p87)

more sedentary pursuits, Beyoğlu also has cinemas, nargileh spots, *hamams* (bathhouses) and more.

☆ AFM FİTAŞ *Cinema*
☎ 212-251 2020; İstiklal Caddesi 24-26; tickets TL12; 🚇 Kabataş then funicular to Taksim Square
Blockbusters. Don't say you weren't warned.

☆ ARAF *Club*
☎ 212-244 8301; 5th fl, Balo Sokak 32; no cover charge; 🕙 5pm-4am; 🚇 Kabataş then funicular to Taksim Square
Grungy fun-central for English teachers and Turkish-language

students, who shake their booties to the in-house Gypsy band and swill the cheapest club beer in town.

☆ BABYLON
Club, Live Music
☎ 212-292 7368; www.babylon.com.tr; Şehbender Sokak 3, Tünel; cover charge varies; 🕙 9.30pm-2am Tue-Thu, 10pm-3am Fri & Sat, closed summer; 🚇 Karaköy then funicular to Tünel
These days, Babylon devotes itself almost exclusively to live performances, and the eclectic program often features big-name international acts. DJ chill-out sessions are in the restaurant-lounge

behind the concert hall. Purchase your tickets at the **box office** (⏲ 10am-6pm) opposite the venue.

☆ DOGZTAR *Live Music*
☎ 212-244 9147; www.dogzstar.com; **3rd fl, Kartal Sokak 3, Galatasaray; cover charge TL5;** ⏲ **closed Sun;** 🚇 **Kabatas, then funicular to Taksim Square**
Its compact size (300 persons max) makes this attitude-free place an acoustic powerhouse. There's a terrace for cooling off in summer.

☆ JOLLY JOKER BALANS
Live Music
☎ 212-251 7762; www.jollyjokerbalans .com; **Balo Sokak 22; admission varies;** ⏲ **closed summer, from 10pm Wed-Sat rest of year;** 🚇 **Kabatas, then funicular to Taksim Square**
The gig-goers among the Joker's lively multinational crowd enjoy the city's best locally brewed beer (the caramel brew) and gravitate towards the upstairs bi-level performance hall, which features an open-air balcony with glass floors. There's live music every night – sometimes in the form of cover bands – and a sound system that's about the best in town.

☆ GHETTO
Live Music
☎ 212-251 7501; www.ghettoist.com; **Kamer Hatun Caddesi 10; cover charge varies;** ⏲ **8pm-4am, closed summer;**

🚇 **Kabatas, then funicular to Taksim Square**
This three-storey club behind the Çiçek Pasajı (p71) has a bold postmodern decor and an interesting musical program featuring local and international acts. Its popular Ghetto Teras (reached via a back staircase) is an open-air restaurant-cum-music-lounge that 'doesn't close until the sun is up'.

☆ HACO PULO
Nargileh & Tea Garden
☎ 212-244 4210; **Hacopolo Pasajı, Galatasaray;** ⏲ **9am-11pm;** 🚇 **Kabataş then funicular to Taksim Square**
There aren't nearly as many traditional teahouses in Beyoğlu as there are in the atmospheric Old City, so this one is treasured by the locals. Set in a delightfully picturesque cobbled courtyard, its stool-to-stool 20- to 30-somethings on summer evenings. Walking from İstiklal Caddesi through the skinny arcade crowded with offbeat shops adds to the experience.

☆ MUNZUR CAFE & BAR
Live Music
☎ 212-244 6327; www.munzurcafebar .com; **Hasnun Galip Sokak 21;** ⏲ **1pm-4am daily, music from 9pm;** 🚇 **Kabatas, then funicular to Taksim Square**
This popular bar in İstanbul's most famous street of *Türkü evlerı*

(Turkish folk music venues) hosts top-notch singers, *bağlama* (lute) players and other musicians.

⭐ **NARDIS JAZZ CLUB**
Jazz
☎ 212-244 6327; www.nardisjazz.com; Galata Kulesi Sokak 14, Galata; cover charge varies; ⏰ 8pm-1am Mon-Thu, to 2am Fri & Sat; 🚋 Karaköy then funicular to Tünel

Just downhill from the Galata Tower, this venue run by jazz guitarist Önder Focan and his wife Zuhal is where real jazz aficionados go. It's small, so you'll need to book if you want a decent table.

⭐ **PERLA KALLÂVİ NARGILEH CAFE** *Nargileh Cafe*
☎ 212-244 9154; 4th-6th fl, Kallâvi Sokak 2; ⏰ 10am-2am; 🚋 Karaköy then funicular to Tünel

Head to the top three floors of this ornate building on İstiklal Caddesi (enter from the side street) to enjoy a tea and nargileh in the welcoming indoor spaces or on

the small terrace with its Sea of Marmara views.

⭐ **ROXY** *Club, Live Music*
☎ 212-249 1283; www.roxy.com.tr, in Turkish; Aslan Yatağı Sokak 5, Taksim; cover charge varies; ⏰ 9pm-3am Wed & Thu, 10pm-4am Fri & Sat; 🚋 Kabataş then funicular to Taksim Square

It has been going since 1994, but the bright young things still flock to this dance-and-performance space off Taksim Square. Expect anything from retro to rap, hip-hop to jazz fusion and electronica.

⭐ **TOPHANE NARGİLEH CAFES** *Nargileh Cafes*
off Necatibey Caddesi, Tophane; 🚋 Tophane

This atmospheric row of nargileh cafes behind the Nusretiye Mosque is always packed with trendy teetotallers. Follow your nose to find it – the smell of apple tobacco is incredibly enticing. For tips on what to do while there, see p138.

>NİŞANTAŞI & AROUND

If you're a dab hand at air kissing and latte drinking, you'll feel totally at home here. Serious shoppers, visiting celebs, PR professionals and the city's gilded youth gravitate towards this upmarket enclave, which is located about 2km north of Taksim Square. Bars, restaurants, boutique hotels and international fashion and design outlets are found in the streets surrounding the main artery, Teşvikiye Caddesi, leading some locals to refer to this enclave as Teşvikiye. Closer to Taksim are the suburbs of Elmadağ and Harbiye, accessed via frantically busy Cumhuriyet Caddesi, where many of the city's airlines are located. To get here, walk or catch the metro from Taksim.

NİŞANTAŞI & AROUND

⊙ SEE
Military Museum **1** B2

🛍 SHOP
Ark Line **2** C1
Beymen **3** C2
Elacindoruk
  Nazanpak **4** C2
Gönül Paksoy **5** C2

Paşabahçe **6** C1
Yargıcı **7** C1

🍴 EAT
Hünkar **8** B1
Kantin **9** C1
Komşu **10** B2
Köşebaşı **11** C3
Zazie **12** C2

🍸 DRINK
Buz Bar **13** C2
Zihni **14** B1

⭐ PLAY
Al Jamal **15** C3
Citylife Cinema **16** C1
Love Dance
  Point **17** B2

👁 SEE
👁 MILITARY MUSEUM

Askeri Müze; ☎ 212-233 2720;
Vali Konağı Caddesi, Harbiye; adult/
student TL4/1; 🕙 9am-5pm Wed-Sun;
🚋 Kabataş then funicular to Taksim
Square & metro to Osmanbey

This sprawling museum located
1km north of Taksim Square will
be of most interest to military
buffs, though children seem to
adore the Çannakale and Conquest dioramas and the displays
of weaponry. Don't miss the
concert by the Mehter, Turkey's
marching military band, which
occurs between 3pm and 4pm
most days.

🛍 SHOP
🛍 ARK LINE *Clothing*

☎ 212-225 9456; www.ark-istanbul.
com; Ihlamur Yolu 5, Teşvikiye;
🕙 10am-7pm Mon-Sat; 🚋 Kabataş
then funicular to Taksim then metro to
Osmanbey

Claiming responsibility for
introducing ethno-chic styles
to İstanbul, this store creates
its own line of casual fashion
ensembles for women, some of
which reference Ottoman styles.
Prices here are less expensive
than usual in this ritzy area, and
the clothes have been designed
to suit women of, as they say, a
certain age.

🛍 BEYMEN
Clothing, Homewares

☎ 212-373 4800; www.beymen.com
.tr; Abdi İpekçi Caddesi 23, Nişantaşı;
🕙 10am-8pm Mon-Sat, noon-8pm Sun;
🚋 Kabataş then funicular to Taksim
then metro to Osmanbey

İstanbul's most glamorous department store stocks European
designer labels aplenty, as well as
stylish homewares in the Bostan
Sokak annexe. The Beymen
Brasserie, with its streetside tables,
is a popular meeting place for
local socialites.

🛍 ELACİNDORUK
NAZANPAK
Jewellery

☎ 212-232 2664; www.elacindoruk
nazanpak.com; Atiye Sokak 14, Teşvikiye;
🕙 2-7pm Mon, 10.30am-7pm Tue-Sat;
🚋 Kabataş then funicular to Taksim
then metro to Osmanbey

It may be small in size, but this
boutique is certainly well endowed when it comes to style. It
showcases contemporary pieces
in silver, gold and other materials.

🛍 GÖNÜL PAKSOY
Clothing

☎ 212-261 9081; Atiye Sokak 6/A &
3, Teşvikiye; 🕙 10am-7pm Mon-Sat;
🚋 Kabataş then funicular to Taksim
Square & metro to Osmanbey

Gönül Paksoy creates and sells
pieces that transcend fashion and

See and be seen at the Beymen Brasserie (p96)

step into art. In fact, her work was the subject of a 2007 exhibition at İstanbul's Rezan Haş Gallery. These two shops showcase her distinctive clothing, which is made using naturally dyed fabrics and is often decorated with vintage beads. Paksöy also creates and sells delicate silk and cotton knits and exquisite jewellery based on traditional Ottoman designs.

PAŞABAHÇE
Glassware

☎ 212-233 5005; Teşvikiye Caddesi 117, Teşvikiye; 🕙 10am-8pm; 🚇 Kabataş then funicular to Taksim Square & metro to Osmanbey

The Teşvikiye branch of the popular local brand (see also p80).

YARGICI
Clothing

☎ 212-225 2952; Vali Konaği Caddesi 30, Teşvikiye; 🕙 9.30am-7.30pm Mon-Sat, 1-6pm Sun; 🚇 Kabataş then funicular to Taksim Square & metro to Osmanbey

Whether they're aged 15 or 50, gals in İstanbul love buying clothes, toiletries and accessories at Yargıcı. The clothes are affordable high-street styles that are made in Turkey and the accessories are so good they're exported internationally.

NEIGHBOURHOODS

NIŞANTAŞI & AROUND

🍴 EAT

🍴 HÜNKAR
Anatolian $$

☎ 212-225 4665; Mim Kemal Öke Caddesi; 🕐 noon-midnight; 🚇 Kabataş then funicular to Taksim Square & metro to Osmanbey

After a morning spent abusing your credit card in nearby shops, you'll be ready to claim a table at this upmarket *lokanta* (eatery serving ready-made food) and enjoy a relaxed lunch. The chefs take enormous pride in cooking and presenting traditional foods supremely well – everything is delicious.

🍴 KANTİN
Modern Turkish $$

☎ 212-219 3114; www.kantin .biz; Akkavak Sokağı 30, Nişantaşı; 🕐 9am-11.30pm Mon-Sat; 🚇 Kabataş then funicular to Taksim then metro to Osmanbey

Flying the flag for the international Slow Food philosophy is Şemsa Denizsel's chic eatery, Kantin. The delicious menu changes daily according to the availability of fresh produce and will please all palates.

🍴 KOMŞU
Kebaps $$

☎ 212-224 9666; www.komsu-kebap .com; Işık Apt, Valı Konağı Caddesi 8, Nişantaşı; 🕐 noon-midnight Mon-Sat;

🚇 Kabataş then funicular to Taksim then metro to Osmanbey

Powerbrokers, professionals and cashed-up locals fill the indoor dining space and pleasant terrace of this kebap restaurant most nights of the week, inevitably leaving happy and replete. The food here is top quality – the house speciality is the meltingly tender *küşleme kebap,* which is made with lamb fillet, but all of the meat dishes are good. It's an easy walk from Taksim Square.

🍴 KÖŞEBAŞİ
Kebaps $$

☎ 212-230 3868; www.kosebasi.com.tr; Bronz Sokak 5, Maçka; 🕐 noon-11pm; 🚇 Kabataş then funicular to Taksim then metro to Osmanbey

Regularly voted one of the best restaurants in town, this long-standing favourite is known for its succulent grills and flavoursome salads. Book ahead.

🍴 ZAZİE *Italian* $$

☎ 212-231 8781; www.zazie.com.tr; Ak Apartımanı, Atiye Sokak 7, Teşvikiye; 🕐 10am-midnight Mon-Sat; 🚇 Kabataş then funicular to Taksim then metro to Osmanbey

This bustling trattoria won *TimeOut Istanbul*'s Best New Restaurant award in 2007 and has been full to the brim ever since. Excellent thin-crust pizzas,

Saffet Emre Tonguç
Professional guide and author (with Pat Yale) of Istanbul: The Ultimate Guide

Most fascinating aspect of the city? Its multicultural heritage. **Is this a living heritage?** İstanbul was cosmopolitan in the past and minorities could easily thrive, but over the past 50 years most neighbourhoods have become very homogenous and the city less cosmopolitan. For instance, although there are 96 Greek Orthodox churches in the city, nearly all are closed year-round. **Do minorities live in particular neighbourhoods?** Jews live in Ulus, in Gayrettepe and around Bağdat St on the Anatolian side. Armenians live in Kurtuluş Şişli, Samatya and Yeşilköy. Only 1800 Greeks are left in the city and they are scattered around Taksim Square and Arnavutköy. **How can travellers get a feel for this heritage?** Go to a restaurant! The Jewish restaurant Levi (☎ 0212 512 1196; Kalçın Sokak 23, Eminönü; ✆ noon-3pm Mon-Fri) still functions and Boncuk (p81) is Armenian-owned. Despina in Kurtuluş (p82) is considered to be one of the best Greek tavernas, but isn't necessarily frequented by community members.

an impressive list of wines by the glass and casual-chic decor give it the winning edge.

🍸 DRINK

🍸 BUZ BAR Bar

☎ 212-291 0065; 2nd fl, Abdi İpekçi Caddesi 42, Teşvikiye; 🕐 4pm-midnight Mon-Thu, 4pm-2am Fri & Sat; 🚇 Kabataş then funicular to Taksim Square & metro to Osmanbey

The music here is a mish-mash of house, R&B and pop, and the crowd is equally mixed – visitors rub shoulders with young entrepreneurs, ad execs and their associates. Drinks are pricey.

🍸 ZİHNİ Bar

☎ 212-248 8033; http://zihnibar.biz; Vali Konağı Caddesi 39; 🕐 6pm-1am Mon-Thu, 6pm-2am Fri & Sat Oct-Apr; 🚇 Kabataş then funicular to Taksim Square & metro to Osmanbey

When antique dealer Zihni Şardağ acquired the fittings of the Park Hotel's historic American Bar in the 1980s, he found himself loathe to part with them. His solution was to open this atmospheric bar in a century-old apartment designed by the famous İstanbullu architect, Vedad Tek. The scene here is elegant and upmarket, as befits its pedigree.

⭐ PLAY

⭐ AL JAMAL
Club

☎ 212-236 5017; Taşkisla Caddesi 3, Maçka Parkı; meal, drinks & entertainment TL175; 🕐 8pm-midnight Mon-Sat;

WORTH THE TRIP

Two tempting shopping experiences are within easy reach of Nişantaşı:

> The best of İstanbul's rapidly expanding portfolio of modern shopping malls, **İstinye Park** (☎ 212-345 5555; İstinye Bayın Caddesi, İstinye; www.istinyepark.com.tr; 🕐 10am-10pm; 🚇 Kabataş then funicular to Taksim then metro to İTÜ Ayazağa) is home to classy department stores Beymen and Vakko, a slew of prestige international designers, high street chains and more.

> Ritzy **Kanyon** (☎ 212-353 5300; www.kanyon.com.tr; Büyükdere Caddesi 185, Levent; 🕐 10am-10pm; 🚇 Kabataş then funicular to Taksim Square & metro to Levent) is the most glamorous shopping mall in town. Multinational names such as Harvey Nichols were quick to sign up when the futuristic building in upmarket Levent opened, ensuring that high-profile local names such as Vakko followed their lead. When there, check out Ottoman Empire, a funky boutique selling T-shirts screenprinted with Ottoman-influenced motifs. From the metro, stay underground and follow the 'Gültepe' signs.

NEIGHBOURHOODS

NİŞANTAŞI & AROUND

🚋 **Kabataş then funicular to Taksim Square then walk**
Drag queens, divas and daddy's darlings all adore Al Jamal. It's kitsch, decadently enjoyable and ruinously expensive – consider yourself warned. Owner Izzet Çapa is the city's most successful nightclub entrepreneur.

⭐ **CITYLIFE CINEMA** *Cinema*
☎ 212-373 3535; www.citylifecinema .com, in Turkish; 6th fl, City's Nişantaşı, Teşvikiye Caddesi 162, Teşvikiye; tickets TL11-15; 🚋 Kabataş then funicular to Taksim Square & metro to Osmanbey
The bar with its magnificent Bosphorus view makes this new multiplex the sexiest cinema in town. It screens a mixed program of arthouse and blockbuster flicks.

⭐ **LOVE DANCE POINT**
Gay Club
☎ 212-296 3357; www.lovedance point.com; Cumhuriyet Caddesi 349, Harbiye; admission free; 🕙 11.30pm-4am Wed, 11.30pm-5am Fri & Sat; 🚋 Kabataş then funicular to Taksim Square then walk
The major player in the city's gay club scene, Love is now in its tenth year and shows absolutely no sign of having its star wane. Here gay anthems meet hard-hitting techno and Turkish pop, making for one hell of a party. Straights can occasionally be spotted on the dance floor.

>BEŞİKTAŞ & ORTAKÖY

This part of town witnessed the waning of the Ottoman Empire. It's full of grandiose palaces and pavilions that the last sultans built in a vain attempt to convince both their subjects and foreign powers of their continuing power, wealth and influence. Alas, Dolmabahçe and Çırağan Palaces did more to destroy the empire than prop it up, sending the treasury into the red and speeding the dynasty's demise. Today, the Bosphorus shoreline between Ortaköy and Kuruçeşme is known for its golden mile of trendsetting restaurants, clubs and cafes. More prosaically, it's also known for its appalling traffic jams – so don't catch a taxi to get here. To see Dolmabahçe Palace or attend a football match at BJK İnönü Stadium, catch the tram to Kabataş (Map pp72–3, G2) and walk the rest of the way. To visit Ortaköy or Kuruçeşme, catch the tram and then a bus down narrow Dolmabahçe/Beşiktaş/Çırağan/Muallim Naci Caddesi.

BEŞİKTAŞ & ORTAKÖY

🅞 SEE
Dolmabahçe
  Palace **1** B4

🏃 DO
Çırağan Palace
  Hotel Kempinski
  Pool **2** D3

🛍 SHOP
Haremlique 3 B3

🍴 EAT
Banyan 4 E4
House Café 5 E4
Park Fora 6 F1
Vogue 7 A3

⭐ PLAY
Anjelique 8 E4
Blackk 9 F1
Crystal 10 F2
İstanbul Jazz
  Center 11 E4
Reina 12 F2
Sortie 13 F1
Supperclub ....(see 10)

👁 SEE
👁 DOLMABAHÇE PALACE

Dolmabahçe Sarayı; ☎ **212-236 9000;**
www.millisaraylar.gov.tr; Dolmabahçe
Caddesi, Beşiktaş; admission adult/child
TL20/1; 🕐 **9am-6pm Tue, Wed & Fri-Sun**
Mar-Sep, 9am-3pm Tue, Wed & Fri-Sun
Oct-Feb; 🚇 **Kabataş then walk**

In 1843 Sultan Abdül Mecit decided that it was time to disprove talk of Ottoman military and financial decline. He chose to do so by commissioning imperial architects Nikoğos and Garabed Balyan to design and build a lavish European-style palace on the shores of the Bosphorus. Interiors were done by the designer of the Paris Opera and have the wow factor in spades. To see the Harem (imperial family quarters) or Selamlık (ceremonial rooms) you must join a guided tour in English or Turkish – sadly, these are often rushed.

🛍 SHOP
HAREMLIQUE
Homewares

☎ **212-236 3843; www.haremlique**
.com; Şair Nedim Bey Caddesi 11,
Akaretler; 🕐 **Mon-Sat;** 🚇 **Kabataş**
then walk

The shops around the fashionable W Istanbul hotel are among the most glamorous in the city. Marni, Chloé, Marc Jacobs and Jimmy Choo are just a few of the labels that draw the city's moneyed elite here to shop. Among these international labels is this local business, which sells top-drawer bedlinen and bathwares. Come here to source items such as luxe *hamam* (bathhouse) accessories including soaps, towels and robes or boudoir cushion-covers featuring Ottoman rococo prints.

Dolmabahçe Palace – one of İstanbul's jewels

🏃 DO

🏃 ÇIRAĞAN PALACE HOTEL KEMPINSKI POOL

Swimming Pool

☎ 212-326 4646; www.kempinski
.com; Çırağan Caddesi 32, Beşiktaş; day
pass weekdays/weekends €100/160;
🕑 7am-7pm; 🚌 Kabataş then bus 22,
22RE or 25E

Nursing a mega-pricey drink
while sitting at one of the
Çırağan's terrace tables and
watching the scene around the
city's best swimming pool, which
is right on the Bosphorus, will
make you feel like Diane Fossey
observing her chimps. Regulars
here share some habits with us
mere mortals, but are definitely a
different species…

🍴 EAT

🍴 AŞŞK KAHVE

Turkish $$

Off Map p103; ☎ 212-265 4734;
Muallim Naci Caddesi 64B, Kuruçeşme;
🕑 9am-10pm, closed Mon in winter;
🚌 Kabataş then bus 22 or 25E

The city's glamour set loves this
garden cafe to bits, and its week-
end brunches are an institution.
Go early if you want to snaffle a
table by the water, and don't
forget to have a botox shot before
you go – that way you'll fit in
nicely. It's accessed via the stairs
behind the Macrocenter.

🍴 BANYAN

Asian $$$

☎ 212-259 9060; www.banyan
restaurant.com; 3rd fl, Salhane Sokak
3, Ortaköy; 🕑 11am-midnight;
🚌 Kabataş then bus 22, 22RE or 25E

The Asian food served at this stylish eatery isn't quite as impressive
as its location overlooking the
Bosphorus Bridge and Ortaköy
Mosque, but the view alone makes
a visit well worthwhile. Phone
ahead to book a table on the
terrace.

🍴 HOUSE CAFÉ

International $$

☎ 212-261 5818; İskele Square 42,
Ortaköy; 🕑 noon-2am; 🚌 Kabataş
then bus 22, 22RE or 25E

This casually chic cafe is one of
the best spots in town for Sunday
brunch. A huge space right on the
waterfront, it offers a good-quality
buffet spread for TL45 between
9am and 2pm. Food at other times
can be disappointing, though that
doesn't deter the locals, who flock
here every weekend.

🍴 PARK FORA

Fish $$$

☎ 212-265 5063; www.parkfora.com;
Muallim Naci Caddesi 54, Kuruçeşme;
🕑 noon-midnight; 🚌 Kabataş then
bus 22 or 25E

This posh waterfront restaurant
in Cemil Topuzlu Parkı serves

truly excellent fish and seafood. If you're after innovative cuisine or super-stylish decor, don't look here – Park Fora is all about classic Turkish dishes cooked using the best quality ingredients on the market and served in conservative but welcoming surrounds.

🍴 VOGUE
International $$$

☎ 212-227 4404; www.istanbuldoors.com; 13th fl, A Blok, BJK Plaza, Spor Caddesi, Akaretler, Beşiktaş; ⓨ noon-2am; 🚇 Kabataş then walk

It seems as if Vogue has been around for almost as long as the Republic. In fact, this sophisticated bar-restaurant in an office block in Beşiktaş opened just over a decade ago. It's a favourite haunt of the Nişantaşı powerbroker

HOME-GROWN HEROES
Beşiktaş gives its name to one of the 'Big Three' football (soccer) teams in İstanbul. Known as the Black Eagles (team colours are black and white), the team's home ground is BJK İnönü Stadium, opposite Dolmabahçe Palace. The Black Eagles' major rivals are the Golden Canaries (Fenerbahçe) and the Lions (Galatasaray). To see a match while you're in town, buy tickets at **Biletix** (www.biletix.com) or at the stadium two to three hours before the game.

set, who love nothing more than enjoying a drink at the terrace bar before moving into the restaurant for pricey sushi or Mod Med dishes.

⭐ PLAY

İstanbul has a killer nightlife, and the best venues are clustered in what is known as the 'Golden Mile' between Ortaköy and Kuruçeşme on the Bosphorus. This sybaritic strip is where world-famous clubs such as Reina and Sortie are located, and it's also where the city's jazz scene has recently started to gravitate. To visit any of the venues listed here, you'll need to dress to kill and be prepared to outlay loads of lira (drinks start at TL20 for a beer and climb into the stratosphere for imported spirits or cocktails). Booking for the restaurants at these venues is a good idea, because it's usually the only way to get past the door staff – otherwise you'll be looking at a lucky break or a tip of at least TL100 to get the nod.

⭐ ANJELIQUE
Club

☎ 212-237 2844; www.istanbuldoors.com; Salhane Sokak 5, Ortaköy; cover charge varies; ⓨ 6pm-4am May-Oct; 🚇 Kabataş then bus 22, 22RE or 25E

Watch boats ply the Bosphorus from your eyrie at Vogue (p106)

The cleverly positioned angled mirrors make the most of Anjelique's location right on the waterfront, ensuring that the few corners of the club without views of the Bosphorus Bridge and Ortaköy Mosque still bathe in their reflections. This is glam with a capital G – wear your Blahniks and be sure to make a reservation.

☆ BLACKK *Club*
☎ 212-236 7256; www.blackk.net, in Turkish; Muallim Naci Caddesi 71, Kuruçeşme; cover charge varies; ⏲ 7.30pm-4am Fri & Sat Nov-Apr; 🚃 Kabataş then bus 22 or 25E

This ultra-fashionable supper club is divided into three areas – club, resto-lounge and the Levendiz Rom (Gypsy) Meyhane. In the summer months, the action moves from this venue into the ultra-fashionable Sortie (p109), one of the two major superclubs on the Golden Mile.

☆ CAUDALIE VINOTHÉRAPIE SPA *Spa*
Off Map p103; ☎ 212-359 1533; www .lesottomans.com.tr; Hotel Les Ottomans, Muallim Naci Caddesi 68, Kuruçeşme; massages TL120-290, treatment packages TL470-715; 🚃 Kabataş then bus 22 or 25E

Barbara Nadel
Author of the Çetin İkmen series of crime novels set in İstanbul

Most of your 13 İkmen novels are set in İstanbul, and are evocative of the city, particularly its Ottoman heritage. Do you think this period was the greatest in the city's history? I think that so far it has proved the most influential. I love its 'take' on 19th-century Parisian style and I enjoy wandering the winding streets of Beyoğlu, Galata and Tarlabaşı admiring their faded splendour and hidden gems. **Do the Ottoman era's social and cultural influences linger?** Most certainly. Many of the rules and stock phrases that define social interaction originate from that time. **Your favourite Ottoman building?** The Süleymaniye Mosque (p18 and p55). And I also like the little-known 18th-century *Yılanlı Yalı* (Mansion of the Snakes) in Bebek. Sultan Mahmud II apparently liked this building so much, its owner had to pretend it was infested with snakes in order to hang on to it!

If you ask the local ladies who lunch to recommend the best spa in town, they almost always nominate this luxurious place in the basement of the Hotel Les Ottomans. The surrounds are exquisite and the therapists are top-notch.

☆ CRYSTAL
Club

☎ 212-261 1988 (ext 2); Muallim Naci Caddesi 65, Ortaköy; adult/student incl 1 drink TL35/25; ⏰ midnight-5.30am Fri & Sat; 🚇 Kabataş then bus 22 or 25E

Crystal is home to the city's techno aficionados, who come to appreciate sets put together by some of the best DJs from Turkey and the rest of Europe. There's a great sound system, a crowded dance floor and a lovely covered garden. Best of all is the fact that there's less attitude evident here than at the rest of the Golden Mile clubs.

☆ İSTANBUL JAZZ CENTER
Jazz Club

☎ 212-327 5050; www.istanbuljazz .com; Salhane Sokak 10, Ortaköy; cover varies according to act; ⏰ 9.30pm & 12.30am, closed summer; 🚇 Kabataş then bus 22, 22RE or 25E

Affectionately known as JC's, this is the city's best jazz club. Big-name international acts regularly perform on Friday and Saturday

nights – check the website for details. There's a set dinner menu costing TL60, or you can order à la carte.

☆ REINA
Club

☎ 212-259 5919; www.reina.com.tr; Muallim Naci Caddesi 44, Ortaköy; cover weekends/weekdays TL50/free; ⏰ May-Oct; 🚇 Kabataş then bus 22 or 25E

According to its website, Reina is a place where foreign presidents discuss world issues, business-men sign multimillion-dollar contracts and stars from all over the world party. In fact, it's where Turkey's C-list celebrities congregate, the city's nouveaux riches cavort and an occasional tourist gets past the doorman to ogle the spectacle and the mag-nificent Bosphorus view. Nearby **Sortie** (☎ 212-327 8585; www.sortie .com.tr, in Turkish; Muallim Naci Caddesi 141; ⏰ 6pm-4am May-Oct) offers more of the same. You are highly unlikely to get into either without a din-ner reservation.

☆ SUPPERCLUB
Club

☎ 212-261 1988 (ext 1); www.sup perclub.com; Muallim Naci Caddesi 65, Kuruçeşme; no cover charge; ⏰ 8:30pm-4am Jun-Sep; Ⓞ Kuruçeşme

With an all-white decor and a location close to the Bosphorus,

WORTH THE TRIP

Most İstanbullus refer to the **Princes' Islands** as 'the Islands' (Adalar).

In Byzantine times, refractory princes, deposed monarchs and others who had outlived their roles were interned here. A ferry service from İstanbul was started in the mid-19th century, and the islands became popular summer resorts with the Greek, Jewish and Armenian business communities in Pera (Beyoğlu). Many of the fine Victorian villas built by these wealthy merchants survive today.

At least nine daily ferries run to the islands between 6.50am and 9pm, departing from the Adalar ferry dock at Kabataş (Map pp72–3, G2), opposite the tram stop. The most useful departure times for day-trippers are 8.30am, 9.20am, 10.10am and 10.40am Monday to Saturday and 8.30am, 9am, 9.30am, 10am and 11am Sunday – but timetables change, so check www.ido.com.tr beforehand. The trip takes approximately 1½ hours and costs TL3 to the islands and the same for the return trip; legs between the islands cost TL1.50. The ferry returns from Büyükada at times including 4pm and 5.45pm Monday to Saturday and 4.30pm, 5.05pm and 5.45pm on Sunday, stopping at Heybeliada en route to Kabataş. The last ferry of the day leaves Büykada at 7.40pm (9pm on Sunday). Note that the ferries are often terribly overcrowded on summer weekends.

Many day-trippers stay on the ferry until Heybeliada (known as Heybeli), stop there to explore, and then hop on another ferry to Büyükada, where they spend the rest of the afternoon before catching a ferry back to Kabataş.

While on the islands, you can follow one of the many walking trails on offer, hire a bicycle or be driven around in a quaint *fayton* (horse-drawn carriage). These provide the only type of transport. There is a recently opened **Islands Museum** on Büyükada (ask a local to show you the way) and it is sometimes possible to visit Heybeliada's historic **Haghia Triada Greek Orthodox Monastery** (☎ 216-351 8563) and its internationally renowned library – you'll need to book ahead to organise this, though.

For lunch on Büyükada, take a picnic, sample the fresh seafood on offer at the ramshackle **Kiyi Restaurant** (Çiçekli Yali Sokak 2; mains TL22; ☼ summer only) near the ferry terminal, or trek up the hill to the Monastery of St George and eat at its simple **restaurant** (mains TL8-10; ☼ daily Apr-Oct, weekends only Nov-Mar). On Heybeliada, your best bet is **Mavi Restaurant** (Yali Caddesi 29; mains TL14-40; ☼ 24hr), a popular fish restaurant on the main waterfront promenade.

the İstanbul branch of Supperclub has a resort feel. Customers lounge or dine in oversized beach beds in lieu of tables and chairs, enjoying the atmospheric lighting, live shows, movie screens, imported DJ talents and creative cuisine.

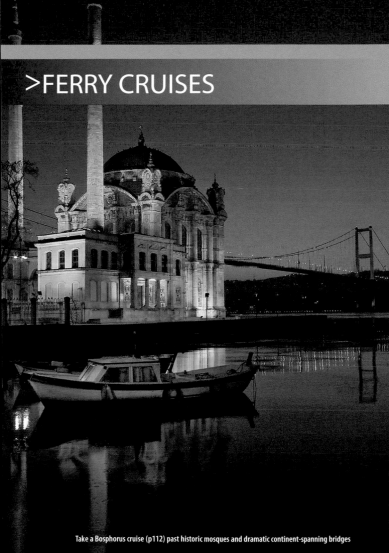

>FERRY CRUISES

Take a Bosphorus cruise (p112) past historic mosques and dramatic continent-spanning bridges

FERRY CRUISES

BOSPHORUS CRUISE

Divan Yolu and İstiklal Caddesi are always awash with people, but neither is the major thoroughfare in İstanbul. That honour goes to the mighty Bosphorus strait, which runs from the Sea of Marmara (Marmara Denizi) to the Black Sea (Karadeniz), located 32km north of the city centre. In modern Turkish, the strait is known as the Boğaziçi or İstanbul Boğazı (from *boğaz*, meaning throat or strait). On one side is Asia, on the other is Europe.

DEPARTURE POINT: EMİNÖNÜ

Hop onto the boat at the Boğaz İskelesi (Bosphorus Public Excursion Ferry Dock) on the Eminönü quay. It's always a good idea to arrive 30 to 45 minutes before the scheduled departure time to be sure of getting a seat with a view. The Asian shore is to the right side of the ferry as it sails up the Bosphorus, the European to the left. As you start your trip up the Bosphorus, you'll see the small island and tower of **Kız Kulesi**, on the Asian side, near Üsküdar. On the European shore, you'll pass grandiose **Dolmabahçe Palace** (p104). In his travelogue *Constantinople in 1890,* French writer Pierre Loti described this and the neighbouring **Çırağan Palace** as '…a line of palaces white as snow, placed at the edge of the sea on marble docks', a description that remains as accurate as it is evocative.

BEŞİKTAŞ TO KANLICA

After a brief stop at Beşiktaş the ferry sails past Çırağan Palace and Ortaköy Square, known for its outdoor eateries and the pretty **Ortaköy Mosque**. Towering over the mosque's minarets is the huge Bosphorus Bridge (Boğaziçi Köprüsü), opened in 1973 on the 50th anniversary of the founding of the Turkish Republic. Just after the bridge, on the Asian side, is **Beylerbeyi Palace** (Beylerbeyi Sarayı; ☎ 216-321 9320; Abdullah Ağa Caddesi; adult/student TL10/1; ⏰ 9.30am-5pm Tue, Wed & Fri-Sun Mar-Sep, to 4pm Tue, Wed & Fri-Sun Oct-Feb). Every sultan needed a little place to escape to, and this 30-room palace was the place for Abdül Aziz (r 1861–76). Look for its two whimsical marble bathing pavilions on the shore, one of which was for men, the other for the women of the harem. The ferry doesn't stop here, but you can visit another time by catching bus 15 from Üsküdar and getting off at the Çayırbaşı stop.

BOSPHORUS CRUISE

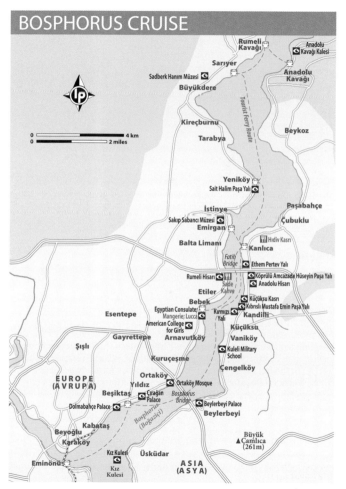

TRANSPORT: BOSPHORUS CRUISE

There are numerous ways to explore the Bosphorus. Most people take the Bosphorus Public Excursion Ferry (one way/return TL15/25), which leaves Eminönü at 10.30am. There are usually extra services at noon and 1.30pm from mid-April to October. These ferries depart from the Boğaz İskelesi (Bosphorus Public Excursion Ferry Dock) at Eminönü and stop at Beşiktaş, Kanlıca, Yeniköy, Sarıyer, Rumeli Kavağı and Anadolu Kavağı. The journey takes 90 minutes each way; return services leave Anadolu Kavağı at 3pm (year-round) and at 4.15pm and 5pm (6pm on Saturday) from mid-April to October. From mid-June to early August, a sunset cruise (TL20) leaves Eminönü on Saturday evenings at 7.15pm and returns from Anadolu Kavağı at 10pm. Check www.ido.com.tr for timetable and fare updates.

Options for exploring by bus are mentioned in the text – a possible itinerary would be to catch the Public Excursion ferry up to Anadolu Kavağı, then take bus 15A to Kanlıca, have lunch at Hıdıv Kasrı and then take bus 15 to Üsküdar, stopping to visit Berlerbeyi Palace on the way. From Üsküdar, it's a pleasant ferry trip back to Eminönü.

Another option is to buy a ticket on a private excursion boat. Although these only take you as far as Anadolu Hisarı and back (without stopping), the fact that the boats are smaller means that you travel closer to the shoreline and so can see a lot more. The whole trip takes about 90 minutes and tickets cost TL10. **Turyol** (☎ 212-512 1287; www.turyol.com) boats leave from the dock on the western side of the Galata Bridge (Galata Köprüsü; next to where the fish sandwiches are sold) every hour from 11am to 6pm on weekdays and every 45 minutes or so from 11am to 7.15pm on weekends. Boats operated by other companies leave from near the Boğaz İskelesi. Bus tickets cost TL1.50 per leg.

Past the suburb of Çengelköy on the Asian side is the imposing **Kuleli Military School**, built in 1860 and immortalised in Irfan Orga's wonderful memoir *Portrait of a Turkish Family*. Look for its two 'witch's-hat' towers.

Almost opposite Kuleli on the European shore is **Arnavutköy**, a suburb boasting a number of well-preserved, frilly Ottoman-era wooden houses, including numerous *yalılar* (waterfront residences; see the boxed text, p116). On the hill above the suburb are buildings formerly occupied by the **American College for Girls**. Its most famous alumna was Halide Edib Adıvar, who wrote about the school in her 1926 autobiography *Memoir of Halide Edib*.

Arnavutköy runs straight into the glamorous suburb of **Bebek**, famous for chic cafes such as **Mangerie** (☎ 212-263 5199; www.mangeriebebek.com; 3rd fl, Cevdetpaşa Caddesi 69; mains TL25-35; ☙ 8am-midnight) and **Lucca** (☎ 212-257 1255; www.luccastyle.com; Cevdetpaşa Caddesi 51b; mains TL20-30; ☙ 10am-2am). As the ferry passes, look out for the mansard roof of the **Egyptian consulate**, an art nouveau mini-palace built by the last Khedive of Egypt, Abbas Hilmi II. It's just south of the waterside park.

Opposite Bebek is **Kandilli**, the 'Place of Lamps', named after the lamps that were lit here to warn ships of the particularly treacherous currents at the headland. Among the many *yalıler* here is the small **Kırmızı Yalı** (Red Yalı), constructed in 1790; a little further on is the long, white **Kıbrıslı Mustafa Emin Paşa Yalı**.

Next to the Kıbrıslı Yalı are the Büyük Göksu Deresi (Great Heavenly Stream) and Küçük Göksu Deresi (Small Heavenly Stream), two brooks that descend from the Asian hills into the Bosphorus. Between them is a grassy, shady delta, which the Ottoman elite thought just perfect for picnics. Foreign residents, who referred to the place as 'the sweet waters of Asia', would often join them. If the weather was good, the sultan joined the party – and did so in style. Sultan Abdül Mecit's version of a picnic blanket was the rococo **Küçüksu Kasrı** (☎ 216-332 3303; Küçüksu Caddesi; adult/ child TL4/2; ⏲ 9.30am-5pm Tue, Wed & Fri-Sun Mar-Sep, to 4pm Tue, Wed & Fri Sun Oct-Feb), constructed from 1856 to 1857. You'll see its ornate cast-iron fence, boat

Pass opulent Dolmabahçe Palace (p104) on a cruise along the Bosphorus

SUMMER RETREATS

The word *yalı* derives from the Greek word for 'coast', and is used to describe the wooden summer residences that were built along the Bosphorus shore by the Ottoman aristocracy and foreign ambassadors in the 17th, 18th and 19th centuries. All are now protected by Turkey's heritage laws.

dock and wedding-cake exterior from the ferry. To visit, get off the ferry at Kanlıca and catch bus 11H or 15F.

On the European side, just before the **Fatih Bridge** (Fatih Köprüsü), the majestic structure of **Rumeli Hisarı** (Fortress of Europe; ☎ 212-263 5305; Yahya Kemal Caddesi 42; admission TL3; ☼ 9am-4.30pm Thu-Tue) looms over a pretty village of the same name. Mehmet the Conqueror had Rumeli Hisarı built in a mere four months during 1452, in preparation for his planned siege of Constantinople. For its location he chose the narrowest point of the Bosphorus, opposite **Anadolu Hisarı** (Fortress of Asia), which had been built by Sultan Beyazıt I in 1391. By doing so, he was able to control all traffic on the strait, thereby cutting the city off from resupply by sea. Just next to the fortress is a clutch of cafes and restaurants, the most popular of which is **Sade Kahve** (☎ 212-358 2324; www.sadekahve.com ; Yahya Kemal Caddesi 36; breakfast plate TL15; ☼ 8am-10pm), a popular weekend brunch spot. To get to Rumeli Hisarı, get off the ferry at Yeniköy or Sarıyer (opposite) and catch bus 25E back towards town. This bus stops at Emirgan (opposite) as well as here at Rumeli Hisarı before terminating at Kabataş.

Almost directly under the Fatih Bridge on the Asian side is the **Köprülü Amcazade Hüseyin Paşa Yalı**. Built right on the water in 1698, it's the oldest *yalı* on the Bosphorus.

KANLICA TO YENİKÖY

Past the bridge, still on the Asian side, is the charming suburb of **Kanlıca**, famous for its rich and delicious yoghurt, which can be sampled at the two cafes in front of the ferry stop or on the ferry itself. This is the ferry's third stop, and if you so choose, you can stop and explore before reboarding the boat on its return trip. From here you can also catch a ferry across to Emirgan or Bebek on the European side and return to town by bus.

High on a promontory above Kanlıca is **Hıdiv Kasrı** (Khedive's Villa; ☎ 216-413 9644; www.beltur.com.tr; Çubuklu Yolu 32, Kanlica; admission free; ☼ 9am-10pm), an exqui-site art nouveau villa built by the last Khedive of Egypt as a summer residence. Restored after decades of neglect, it now functions as a restaurant (mains TL10 to TL20.50) and garden cafe (sandwiches and cakes TL4 to TL6). The villa is a gem, and the extensive garden is superb, particularly during the International İstanbul Tulip Festival (p22) in April. To get here from the ferry stop, turn left into Halide Edip Adıvar Caddesi and then turn right into narrow Kafadar Sokak. Walk all the way up steep Hacı Muhittin Sokağı until you see a sign for Hadiv Kasrı Caddesi – the villa is on the left.

Opposite Kanlıca on the European shore is the wealthy suburb of **Emirgan**. It's well worth visiting for the impressive **Sakıp Sabancı Müzesi** (☎ 212-277 2200; http://muze.sabanciuniv.edu; Sakıp Sabancı Caddesi 42; admission varies according to exhibition; ⏰ 10am-6pm Tue, Thu, Fri-Sun, to 10pm Wed & Sat), which hosts world-class travelling exhibitions. The museum is also home to one of the city's most glamorous eateries, **Müzedechanga** (☎ 212-323 0901; www.changa -istanbul.com; mains TL22-40; ⏰ 10.30am-1am Tue-Sun).

YENİKÖY TO SARIYER

North of Emirgan is **Yeniköy**, on a point jutting out from the European shore. This is the ferry's next stop. First settled in classical times, Yeniköy later became a favourite summer resort, as indicated by **Sait Halim Paşa Yalı**,

Rumeli Hisarı stands sentry over two continents and the Bosphorus' narrowest point

FERRY CRUISES

the lavish 19th-century Ottoman *yalı* of the one-time grand vizier. Look for its two small stone lions on the quay. On the opposite shore is the suburb of **Paşabahçe**, famous for its glassware factory.

Originally called Therapeia for its healthy climate, the little cove of **Tarabya** to the north of Yeniköy on the European shore has been a favourite summer watering place for İstanbul's well-to-do for centuries, although modern development has sullied some of its charm. For an account of Therapeia in its heyday, read Harold Nicholson's 1921 novel *Sweet Waters*.

North of the village are some of the old summer embassies of foreign powers. When the heat and fear of disease increased in the summer months, foreign ambassadors and their staff would retire to these palatial residences, complete with lush gardens. Such residences extended north to the village of **Büyükdere**, also notable for its churches and the **Sadberk Hanım Müzesi** (☎ 212-242 3813; www.sadberkhanimmuzesi.org.tr; Piyasa Caddesi 27-29; admission TL7; ☼ 10am-5pm Thu-Tue), named after the wife of the late Vehbi Koç, founder of Turkey's foremost commercial empire. There's an eclectic collection here, including beautiful İznik and Kütahya ceramics, Ottoman silk textiles, and Roman coins and jewellery. The museum is a 10-minute walk from the next ferry stop, at Sarıyer.

SARIYER TO ANADOLU KAVAĞI

After stopping at Sarıyer, the ferry sails on to **Rumeli Kavağı**, known for its fish restaurants. After a short stop here it then crosses the strait to finish the journey at **Anadolu Kavağı**. Surrounded by countryside, this is a pleasant spot in which to wander and have a seafood lunch, though it's somewhat blighted by the presence of pushy restaurant touts. Perched above the village are the ruins of **Anadolu Kavağı Kalesi** (Yoros Kalesi), a medieval castle that originally had eight massive towers in its walls. First built by the Byzantines, it was restored and reinforced by the Genoese in 1350, and later by the Ottomans. To get there, it's a 25-minute walk up steep Caferbaba Sokağı.

If you decide to travel back to town by bus rather than ferry, catch bus 15A to Beykoz or Kanlıca from the main square and then transfer to bus 15 to Üsküdar or bus E-2 to Taksim.

GOLDEN HORN CRUISE

Most visitors to İstanbul have some awareness or knowledge about the Bosphorus cruise, but not too many have heard about the Golden Horn

(Haliç) trip that is also an option. Until recently, this stretch of water to the north of the Galata Bridge (Galata Köprüsü) was heavily polluted and its suburbs offered little to tempt the traveller. All that's changing these days, though. The waters have been cleaned up, beautification works are under way along the shores, and impressive museums and galleries are opening in the Haliç suburbs. Spending a day hopping on and off the ferry and exploring will give you an insight into a very different – and far less touristy – İstanbul.

GOLDEN HORN CRUISE

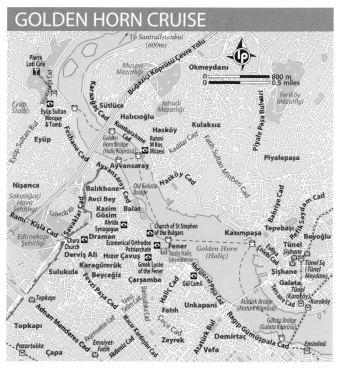

DEPARTURE POINT: EMİNÖNÜ

These ferries start in Üsküdar, on the Asian side, and stop at Karaköy before taking on most of their passengers at the Haliç İskelesi (Golden Horn Ferry Dock) on the far side of the Galata Bridge at Eminönü. The *iskelesi* (dock) is behind a car park next to the Storks jewellery store. The ferry then passes underneath the Atatürk Bridge and stops at Kasımpaşa on the opposite side of the Golden Horn. This area is where the Ottoman imperial naval yards were located, and some of the original building stock is still evident.

FENER

The next disembarkation point is on the opposite shore, at Fener. This area is the traditional home of the city's Greek population, and although few Greeks live in the area these days, a number of important Greek Orthodox sites are located here. The prominent red-brick building on the hill is the **Greek Lycée of the Fener** (Megali School or Great School), the oldest house of learning in İstanbul. The Greek Lycée has been housed in Fener since before the Conquest – the present building dates from 1881.

Closer to the shore, to the left of the ferry stop and across Abdülezel Paşa Caddesi, is the **Ecumenical Orthodox Patriarchate** (☎ 212-531 9670; www .ec-patr.org; Sadrazam Ali Paşa Caddesi; donation requested; 🕒 9am-5pm). The compound is built around the historic Church of St George, which dates from 1730. Every Sunday morning, busloads of Greek Orthodox pilgrims come here for the Divine Liturgy.

TRANSPORT: GOLDEN HORN CRUISE

Haliç ferries leave Eminönü every hour from 7.45am (10.45am on Sundays) to 8pm (9pm on Sundays); the last ferry returns to Eminönü from Eyüp at 7.45pm (8.45pm on Sundays). The ferry trip takes 35 minutes and costs TL1.50 per leg. Check www.ido.com.tr for timetable and fare updates.

If you wish to return by bus rather than ferry, bus 36E, 44B, 99 and 399B travel from outside the ferry stop at Eyüp via Balat and Fener to Eminönü. Buses 39 and 39B travel via Edirnekapı to Beyazıt, allowing you to stop and visit the Chora Church (see the boxed text, p68) on your way back.

To return to Taksim from Hasköy or Sütlüce by bus, catch the 36T or 54HT. For Eminönü, catch the 47, 47Ç or 47E.

All bus tickets cost TL1.50

Sample the less-touristed side of İstanbul with a ferry trip along the Golden Horn (Haliç)

To the right of the ferry stop, in the waterside park, is the attractive Gothic Revival **Church of St Stephen of the Bulgars** (Sveti Stefan Church; Mürsel Paşa Caddesi 85). This cast-iron church was constructed in Vienna, then shipped down the Danube and assembled here in 1871. It's not normally open to visitors, but has in the recent past functioned as a venue for the International İstanbul Music Festival.

If you're hungry, Fener is home to the most famous *işkembecisi* (tripe soup shop) in the city: **Tarihi Haliç İşkembecisi** (☎ 212-534 9414; www.haliciskem becisi.com; Abdülezel Paşa Caddesi 315; ⏾ 24hr). Locals swear by the hangover-fighting properties of *işkembe* (tripe soup) and often make late-night pilgrimages here. It's on the main road opposite the ferry stop.

East of the ferry stop in a bustling neighbourhood shopping strip is the **Gül Mosque** (Gül Camii; crn Gül Camii Sokak & Şerefiye Sokak), an 11th-century building originally known as the Church of St Theodosia. Legend has it that on Theodosia's saint's day (29 May) preceding the Conquest, worshippers filled the church with rose petals in her honour and prayed that the Ottomans wouldn't be successful in breaching the city's walls. Their prayers went unanswered, but when soldiers of Mehmet's army entered they saw the petals and renamed the building Gül (Rose) Mosque. In fact, the building was used as a shipyard warehouse after the Conquest and wasn't converted into a mosque until the reign of Beyazıt II (r 1481–1512). Built to a cross-domed plan, it has a central, extremely high, dome that is an Ottoman addition and a pretty minaret dating from the rule of Selim II (r 1512–20).

To the west of Fener is the slowly gentrifying suburb of Balat, once home to a large proportion of Istanbul's Jewish population and now crowded with migrants from the east of the country. The suburb is home to the city's oldest Jewish house of worship, the **Ahrida Synagogue** (Ahrida Sinagogu; Vodina Caddesi 9), built by Macedonian Jews in the 15th century and given a thorough restoration in the early 1990s. These days the synagogue has a congregation of only 21. Unfortunately, its cantankerous caretaker actively discourages visitors.

HASKÖY TO SÜTLÜCE

Passing the derelict remains of the original Galata Bridge on its journey, the ferry crosses to the opposite shore and stops next at Hasköy, home to

The always-spectacular İstanbul skyline seen at sunset from the Golden Horn

the fascinating **Rahmi M Koç Müzesi** (☎ 212-369 6600; www.rmk-museum.org.tr; Hasköy Caddesi 5; adult/child & student TL11/6, submarine TL6/4; ☼ 10am-5pm Tue-Fri, to 7pm Sat & Sun). Founded by the head of the Koç industrial group to exhibit artefacts from İstanbul's industrial past, this museum is as popular with children as it is with adults and is well worth a visit. It's directly to the left of the ferry stop as you disembark.

The next stop is Ayvansaray on the opposite shore, from where you can get off the ferry and follow the remains of Theodosius II's massive land walls uphill to visit the Chora Church (see the boxed texts, p68).

The ferry then crosses under the Haliç Bridge to Sütlüce. Art-lovers should consider getting off here and catching bus 36T, 47, 47Ç or 47E to Bilgi Üniversitesi, home to **Santralİstanbul** (☎ 212-311 7809; www.santralistanbul .org; Kazım Karabekır Caddesi 2/6, Eyüp; adult/over 65 & under 13/student TL7/5/3; ☼ 10am-8pm Tue-Sun). Housed in a converted power station, it's one of the best contemporary art galleries in the city.

EYÜP

The ferry's last stop is across the water in Eyüp. This conservative suburb is built around the **Eyüp Sultan Mosque & Tomb** (Camii Kebir Sokak; ☼ tombs 9.30am-4.30pm), one of the most important religious sites in Turkey. The tomb supposedly houses the remains of Ayoub al-Ansari (Eyüp Ensari in Turkish), a friend of the Prophet's and a revered member of Islam's early leadership. Eyüp fell in battle outside the walls of Constantinople while carrying the banner of Islam during the Arab assault and siege of the city from 674 to 678. The mosque built next to his tomb was where the Ottoman princes came for their coronations – it was levelled by an earthquake in 1766 and the present mosque was built in its place. To get here, cross the road from the ferry stop and walk up İskele Caddesi, the main shopping street, until you reach the mosque.

After visiting the mosque and tomb, many visitors head north up the hill to enjoy a glass of tea and the wonderful views on offer at the **Pierre Loti Café** (☎ 212-581 2696; Gümüşsuyu Balmumcu Sokak 1, Eyüp; ☼ 8am-midnight), where the famous French novelist is said to have come for inspiration. To get here, walk out of the mosque's main gate and turn right. Walk around the complex (keeping it to your right) until you see a set of stairs and a steep cobbled path winding uphill through the Eyüp Sultan Mezarlığı (Cemetery of the Great Eyüp), burial ground to many important Ottoman figures. Alternatively, a cable car (TL1.50 each way; ☼ 8am-11pm) travels from the waterfront to the top of the hill.

>SNAPSHOTS

There are nearly as many quality accommodation options in İstanbul as there are top-notch eating, drinking, entertainment and shopping opportunities – and the list of attractions doesn't stop there. Add extraordinary architecture, a rich cultural heritage and a vibrant arts scene and you have all the ingredients for a holiday that will be as rewarding as it is relaxing.

A tram whizzes over Galata Bridge (Galata Köprüsü; p52), with the New Mosque (p53) in the background

ACCOMMODATION

Back in the 1970s, when İstanbul was a major stop on the overland hippy trail between Europe and India, the only sleeping options in town were grubby guesthouses clustered around the Blue Mosque (Sultan Ahmet Camii) and Aya Sofya. These offered lumpy mattresses, filthy bed linen and cold-water showers, but the clients weren't fussed – they were all too stoned to notice. Fortunately, there's a new generation of guesthouses in Sultanahmet that couldn't be more different (the same applies to their clients). Most of these places follow the same model, offering clean and compact rooms with a simple but stylish Anatolian-influenced decor. Breakfast is included in the room rate and is often served on a comfortable roof terrace with great views. There are a few exceptions to the rule – myriad backpacker hostels and the luxe **Four Seasons Hotel** (www.fourseasons .com/Bosphorus) being the obvious examples – but on the whole, Sultanahmet is where you should stay if you want a dependable mid-priced option near the major sights.

Although a few Sultanahmet hotels can rightfully claim to be boutique establishments, most hip or designer sleeping options are across the Galata Bridge (Galata Köprüsü). Staying in Beyoğlu, Beşiktaş, Ortaköy or Nişantaşı means that you'll be close to the city's eating, shopping and clubbing scenes, and far away from the tourist touts who work the streets of the Old City. This side of town is also home to a growing number of stylish apartment rentals, the most impressive of which are offered by **Manzara** (www.manzara-istanbul.com/en) and **İstanbul Holiday Apartments** (www.istanbul holidayapartments.com). If you're here primarily to party at the superclubs, the

obvious choice is the comfortable **Radisson SAS Bosphorus Hotel** (www
.radissonsas.com), located in the heart of the Golden Mile in Ortaköy.

Those coming to town for a romantic sojourn should consider staying at
a luxurious boutique hotel housed in a restored *yalı* (waterfront residence)
on the Bosphorus. There are only a few of these – half on the European
side and half on the Asian (Anatolian) side – and they are without doubt
the most atmospheric sleeping options in town, offering unrivalled views,
excellent restaurants and exemplary service. Best of all is the fact that most
have private motor launches that ferry guests up and down the Bosphorus
when they want to leave the seclusion of their drop-dead-gorgeous rooms
and hit the tourist trails. Top picks are **Sumahan on the Water** (www.sumahan.com),
Ajia (www.ajiahotel.com) and **Hotel Les Ottomans** (www.lesottomans.com.tr).

Most hotels drop their rates during low season (October to April, but
not around Christmas or Easter); you should be able to negotiate a discount of at least 20% at these times. Before you confirm any booking, ask
if the hotel will give you a discount for cash payment (usually 10% but
can be higher), whether a pick-up from the airport is included (it often is
if you stay more than three nights) and whether there are discounts for
extended stays. Make sure you book ahead from May to September.

MOST STYLISH MIDRANGE SLEEPS
> 5 Oda (www.5oda.com)
> Ansen 130 Suites (www.ansensuites
  .com)
> Hotel Empress Zoe (www.emzoe.com)
> Hotel Ibrahim Pasha (www.ibrahim
  pasha.com)

BEST VALUE FOR MONEY
> Hanedan Hotel (www.hanedanhotel
  .com)
> Hotel Alp Guesthouse (www.alpguest
  house.com)
> Marmara Guesthouse (www.marmara
  guesthouse.com)
> Istanbul Apartments (www.istanbul
  apt.com)

BEST ROOFTOP TERRACES
> Ararat Hotel (www.ararathotel.com)
> Hotel Anemon Galata (www.anemon
  hotels.com)
> Hotel Sari Konak (www.istanbulhotel
  sarikonak.com)
> İstanbul Hotel Nomade (www.hotel
  nomade.com)

BEST DESIGNER HOTELS
> Four Seasons Istanbul at the Bosphorus
  (www.fourseasons.com/bosphorus)
> The House Hotel and Apartments
  (www.thehousehotel.com)
> Tomtom Suites (www.tomtomsuites
  .com)
> Witt Istanbul Suites (www.wittistan
  bul.com)

SNAPSHOTS

ARCHITECTURE

Urban designers wanting to study best practice when it comes to putting together a city skyline need go no further than İstanbul. Forget Chicago and New York with their skyscrapers, or London with its gimmicky Eye and squat clock tower – İstanbul is the real thing. Here you'll find delicate minarets reaching towards the heavens, distinctive domes crowning hills, and austere and elegant medieval towers with commanding views across the water.

This imperial city is the architectural equivalent of a chocolate box with the best possible assortment of treats – Byzantine cathedrals and churches are located next to Ottoman mosques, *medreseler* (theological schools) and *hamamlar* (bathhouses); distinctive 19th-century timber *yaliler* (waterfront residences) adorn both shores of the Bosphorus; and neoclassical embassy buildings are dotted along Beyoğlu's boulevards. Little of note dates from the second half of the 20th century, so the city is consolidating its time-capsule status, undergoing a continuous program of restoration to preserve its architectural heritage and attempting to enact legislation to protect the revered Stamboul skyline. Time capsule doesn't mean Disney-like, though: İstanbullus still worship in historic mosques, live in timber houses, run restaurants in *medreseler,* sweat out the worries of the week in *hamamlar* and attend cocktail parties in embassies.

Today's İstanbul is a living testimonial to the architects and patrons who have contributed to its contemporary form. It's also proof that back in the old days, they sure knew how to erect great buildings.

The oldest surviving buildings are in the Old City, with a number of Byzantine structures remaining, including churches, cisterns, fortresses and fortified walls. Urban spaces such as the Hippodrome (p38) and ceremonial boulevards such as Divan Yolu also date from this era. In Beyoğlu, traces of the Genoese presence dating back to the final years of the Byzantine Empire can be found, as can buildings from every stage of Ottoman rule. Early essays in the development of a national architectural movement in the early 20th century are found on both sides of the Golden Horn (Haliç). These areas are where most visitors spend their time, but there are discoveries galore through every part of the city. In fact, that's what makes the place so fascinating – the layers of history have a physical manifestation here. There might be stellae from a Roman ceremonial way on one corner and an Ottoman *han* (caravanserai) on another… You'll end up acting like an archaeologist, looking to make new discoveries each time you leave your hotel room.

BEST BYZANTINE BUILDINGS
> Aqueduct of Valens (p52)
> Aya Sofya (p12)
> Basilica Cistern (p37)
> Little Aya Sofya (p52)
> Theodosian Walls (p68)

BEST OTTOMAN BUILDINGS
> Atik Valide Mosque (p48)
> Beylerbeyi Palace (p112)
> Blue Mosque (p37)
> Süleymaniye Mosque (p55)
> Topkapı Palace (p10)

Top left Apartment buildings in Bebek **Above** Elaborate mosaics around the Circumcision Room door at Topkapı Palace (p10)

DRINKING

It may be the biggest city in a predominantly Muslim country, but let us assure you that İstanbul's population likes nothing more than a drink or three – particularly if it's the city's beloved tipple, rakı (aniseed brandy). If the alcohol-soaked atmosphere in the city's *meyhaneler* (taverns) isn't a clear enough indicator, a foray into the thriving bar scene around Beyoğlu will confirm it.

Rakı is something of an acquired taste, but its aniseed tang and fragrant aroma reward perseverance. It should be approached with caution, though, because it packs one heck of a punch and Turks frown upon public displays of drunkenness.

If you feel on safer ground with more familiar tipples, Turkish *şarap* (wine) is improving in quality every year. Look for bottles with the Sarafin, Karma or Doluca Kav Tuğra labels to enjoy the best drinking. If ordering by the glass, ask for *bir bardak beyaz şarap* if you want white, *bir bardak kırmızı şarap* if you want red, and *bir bardak lâl şarap* if you're feeling in the mood for a summery rosé.

Local beers Efes Pilsen and Tuborg are the chilled bevvie of choice in Beyoğlu's bohemian drinking dens, while cocktails are shaken or stirred with gay abandon and a great deal of expertise in the stylish surrounds of the Bosphorus superclubs or at Beyoğlu's rooftop bars.

Alternatively, you could check out the alcohol-free, atmosphere-rich *çay bahçesiler* (tea gardens) dotted around the Old City and join in the national pastime of drinking delicate tulip-shaped glasses of *çay* (tea). Sugar cubes are the only accompaniment and you'll find these are needed to counter the effects of long brewing. Ask for milk and the waiter will respond with either hilarity or incomprehension.

Surprisingly, *Türk kahve* (Turkish coffee) isn't widely consumed. A thick and powerful brew, it's drunk in a couple of short sips. If you order a cup, you will be asked how sweet you like it – *çok şekerli* means 'very sweet', *orta şekerli* 'middling', *az şekerli* 'slightly sweet' and *sade* 'not at all'. It will be accompanied by a glass of water, which is to clear the palate before you sample the delights of the coffee.

Italian-style coffee is another matter entirely. In fact, we will go so far as to say that the city has gone batty over its espresso beans, and really needs to calm down. At the time of research there were seven multinational coffee-chain franchises on İstiklal Caddesi alone. In our view, that's caffeine addiction that's getting truly out of hand…

MOST ATMOSPHERIC TEA & TURKISH-COFFEE STOPS
> Derviş Aile Çay Bahçesi (p49)
> Haco Pulo (p92)
> Şark Kahvesi (p67)
> Set Üstü Çay Bahçesi (p47)
> Yeni Marmara (p49)

BEST ROOFTOP BARS
> 5 Kat (p87)
> 360 (p87)
> Hotel Nomade Terrace Bar (p46)
> Leb-i Derya (p89)
> Mikla (p90)
> X Bar (p90)

Top left Sip apple tea at a *çay bahçesi* **Above** Turkish coffee – you can drink it, or pave roads with it

FOOD

More than anything else, İstanbullus love to eat. Here food is much more than mere fuel. Instead, it's a celebration of community. Meals unfurl with great ceremony – they are joyful, boisterous and almost inevitably communal.

The national cuisine has been refined over centuries and is treated more reverently than any museum collection in the country. That's not to say it's fussy, because what differentiates Turkish food from other national noshes is its rustic and honest base. The meze (hors d'oeuvres) you'll eat will be simple, the kebaps austere, the salads unstructured and the seafood unsauced. Flavours will explode in your mouth because ingredients are used in season – being a locavore is taken for granted here.

The dishes served up in restaurants throughout İstanbul are the same as those served up in eateries around the country in all but one important respect – they're better. This is where the country's best chefs come to perfect their art and where the greatest range of cuisines – both regional and international – are showcased. In Beyoğlu, you're just as likely to encounter an innovative and perfectly executed take on an Italian pasta dish as you are a classic meze selection or a fabulously fresh grilled fish. Feel like sushi or a fragrant Thai red curry? You'll get it here. Have a yen to challenge your tastebuds with an edgy fusion dish conceived and prepared by a European- or Australasian-trained master of the kitchen? No problem – the city has plenty of options.

The city's best eateries are in Beyoğlu. This is where you should come to sample a procession of hot and cold meze dishes in a *meyhane* (tavern), or take your pick from a scrumptious array of Anatolian dishes on display in a *lokanta* (eatery serving ready-made food). It's also where you should come to eat in the city's two best Western-style restaurants: Mikla (p86) and Changa (p83).

Away from Beyoğlu, you should seek out the national dish – kebaps – in Eminönü or further afield or investigate a *balık restoran* (fish restaurant) along the Bosphorus. The possibilities are endless.

As the Turks say, *Afiyet olsun!* (Good appetite!)

BEST MEYHANELER
> Demeti (p82)
> Despina (p82)
> Karaköy Lokantası (p84)
> Sofyalı 9 (p86)

BEST FISH RESTAURANTS
> Balıkçı Sabahattın (p44)
> Doğa Balık (p83)
> Tarıhı Karaköy Balık Lokantası (p86)

BEST LOKANTAS
> Çiya Sofrası (p48)
> Hacı Abdullah (p83)
> Hünkar (p98)

BEST KEBAP RESTAURANTS
> Beyti (p65)
> Develi (p65)
> Hamdi Et Lokantası (p64)
> Köşebaşı (p98)
> Zübeyir Ocakbaşı (p87)

Top left The hustle and bustle of Taksim *meyhaneler* **Above** Who visits İstanbul without sampling a kebap?

SHOPPING

Fill your wallets and charge your credit cards, because İstanbul is a shopa-holic's paradise. It's impossible to explore every bazaar, arcade and mall here, but even a couple of days will be enough to make the dreaded term 'excess baggage' a very real possibility.

Over centuries, İstanbullus have perfected the practice of shopping, and then shopping some more. Trading is in their blood and they've turned making a sale or purchase into a true art form. Go into any carpet shop and you'll see what we mean – you'll find etiquette to be followed, tea to be drunk, conversation to be had. And, of course, there's money to be spent and made.

Whether you're after a cheap souvenir or a family-heirloom-to-be, you'll find it here. Rugs, textiles, ceramics, spices, olive-oil soap and jewel-lery are everywhere, but you can also find fashion and homewares that can hold their own against the stock of any concept store in London, LA or Lisbon.

The Grand Bazaar (Kapalı Çarşı; p52) is the city's most famous place to shop. Come here for jewellery, leather, textiles, rugs and ceramics, but be prepared to sift through the tourist tat for quality items. And don't expect bargains – shop rents are high here, and prices are set accordingly.

The Arasta Bazaar (p40), behind the Blue Mosque in Sultanahmet, is lined with top-quality carpet, textile and ceramic shops – it's a great place to window-shop.

The shopping precinct between the Grand Bazaar and Eminönü (called Tahtakale by locals) is home to the historic Spice Bazaar (Misir Çarşi; p55). It and nearby Hasırcılar Caddesi are where to buy dried fruits, spices and lotions.

Over in Beyoğlu, İstiklal Caddesi (p77) is lined with multinational-brand clothing and shoe shops. A few steps away is the neighbourhood of Çukur-cuma, home to many of the city's best antique and curio shops. The nearby enclaves of Galata and Cihangir are the places to come if you're interested in checking out the boutiques of young fashion designers and jewellers.

Turkey's big fashion names and foreign labels are found in Nişantası and at the Kanyon and İstinye Park shopping malls (p100).

See p58 for a guide to buying carpets and kilims, and p59 for a guide to bargaining.

BEST TEXTILE, CLOTHING & RUG BUYS

> Contemporary kilims (pileless woven rugs) from Dhoku (p60)
> Modern Turkish fashion from Gönül Paksoy (p96) or Doors (p78)
> Rugs from Cocoon (p40) and Mehmet Çetinkaya Gallery (p42)
> *Suzani* bedspreads from Muhlis Günbatti (p60)

BEST ART, ANTIQUE & JEWELLERY BUYS

> Gold jewellery from Sofa (p62) and Phebus (p62)
> *Lale* (tulip) motif necklaces and earrings from Design Zone (p59)
> Miniature paintings from Artrium (p78)
> Russian icons and Turkish calligraphy from Khaftan (p42)

BEST HANDICRAFT BUYS

> Cotton and linen peştemalar (bath towels) from Abdulla Natural Products (p57), Derviş (p59), Yılmaz İpekçilik or Jennifer's Hamam (p42)
> Felt jewellery, dolls and hats from Cocoon (p40) or Ak Gümüş (p57)
> Hand-painted ceramic platters and bowls from İznik Classics & Tiles (p41) or SIR (p80)
> Olive-oil soap from Abdulla Natural Products (p57) or Derviş (p59)

BEST FOOD & DRINK BUYS

> Baklava from Karaköy Güllüoğlu (p84)
> Dried fruit from Malatya Pazarı (p60)
> *Lokum* (Turkish delight) from Ali Muhiddin Hacı Bekir (p57) or Hafız Mustafa Şekerlemeleri (p64)
> Spices from the Spice Bazaar (p55)

Above Treat your feet to one of the colourful carpets at the Grand Bazaar's Nuruosmaniye entrance

GAY & LESBIAN

It wasn't too long ago that İstanbul's gay and lesbian scene was strictly furtive and somewhat dull. Fortunately, recent years have seen it becoming increasingly accepted and dynamic. In many ways it's similar to the scenes in other major European capitals, the only differences being that there are more tranny bars here and fewer leather and fetish clubs. Check www.istanbulgay.com for a general guide.

There seems to be a hot new gay bar or club opening in Beyoğlu every week, mainly around the Taksim Square end of İstiklal Caddesi. Long-standing favourites include Club 17 (p89) and Love Dance Point (p101), but many others are listed in the Gay & Lesbian section in the monthly magazine *TimeOut İstanbul* (www.timeoutistanbul.com).

There's an excellent gay-owned-and-run hotel in Beyoğlu called **Eklektik Guesthouse** (Map pp72-3, C4; ☎ 212-243 7446; www.eklektikgalata.com; Kadrıbey Cıkmazi 4, Galata; r €95-125; 🗶 🔀 💻), and a Sultanahmet-based tour company specialising in gay travel called **Pride Travel** (Map p35, B4; ☎ 212-527 0671; www.turkey-gay -travel.com; 2nd fl, Ateş Pasaji, İncili Cavus Sokak 33, Sultanahmet; 🕙 10am-6pm Mon-Sat).

Hamams have been a gay fave, but in recent years this has changed. Journalist René Ames, who writes *Time Out*'s gay and lesbian section, says Police have been pretty vigilant against lewdness in *hamams* recently, so much so that bathhouse habitué's say that the traditional homoerotic undercurrents in these bathhouses have changed considerably.' He identifies Yeşildırek Hamamı (p77) as being one of the few gay *hamams* to continue to operate despite the current climate, but cautions visitors to be discreet.

A gay-pride march temporarily redecorates İstiklal Caddesi

HAMAMS

You've probably heard of Jerusalem syndrome, but did you know İstanbul has an equivalent? In this phenomenon, millions of visitors each year take off their clothes in public almost as soon as they arrive in the city. The reason? To enjoy the delights of the *hamam* (bathhouse), of course.

The popular choice for a first-time *hamam* experience is usually one of the 'big two' – Cağaloğlu Hamamı (p40) and Çemberlitaş Hamamı (p56). Though touristy, these offer gorgeous Ottoman surrounds and are places where most of the clientele will also be having their first experience of a *hamam*, so you won't feel out of place.

What should you expect when you cross the threshold? You'll enter the *camekan* (dressing room), where you undress, store your clothes and valuables, wrap the provided *peştemal* (bath towel) around you and don a pair of *nalın* (sandals). An attendant will then lead you to the heart of the *hamam*: the *sıcaklık* (steam room).

It's cheapest to bring along soap, shampoo and cloth and wash yourself, but it's more enjoyable to lie on the *göbektaşı* (hot marble platform) and have an attendant douse you with warm water and then scrub you with a *kese* (coarse cloth mitten). You'll then be lathered with a sudsy swab, shampooed, rinsed off and (if you so choose) massaged.

Bath etiquette dictates that men should keep the *peştemal* on at all times. In the women's section, the amount of modesty expected varies considerably – at tourist *hamams* you can keep your underwear on, wear a bathing suit or bare all. Also see p19.

Steam away your worries and your jetlag at a hamam

KEYİF

Forget the Moonies or Scientology – there's a more powerful cult at work in İstanbul. Followers of *keyif,* the Turkish art of quiet relaxation, are gaining in number every year and seem to have an uncanny knack for drawing unsuspecting visitors into their soporific society.

Notice the old men sitting in front of shops, on doorsteps and on park benches. They're happy to soak up the sun and watch the world go past without reading newspapers, talking politics or listening to an iPod. In short, they're enjoying *keyif*.

The same applies to players of backgammon (pictured below). Tea is drunk and acquaintances are nodded to, but the only sound heard during the game is the melodious clink of checkers and die. It's all about *keyif*.

To see the converted en masse, you need go no further than a *çay bahçesi* (tea garden). Here İstanbullus indulge in the habit of nargileh (water pipe) smoking, aka extreme *keyif*. Beware the comfortable bean-bag seats at the Tophane nargileh cafes (p93) and the shady surrounds of Old City *çay bahçesiler*.

When ordering a nargileh, cult members specify their tobacco of choice. Most opt for wonderfully fragrant *elma* (tobacco cured in apple molasses), but others order their tobacco *tömbeki* (unadulterated). The nargileh is then brought to their table, hot coals are placed in the pipe to get it started, and a disposable plastic mouthpiece is provided to slip over the pipe's stem. After inhaling gently, the water in the *gövde* (body) bubbles and total *keyif*ication ensues. Consider yourselves warned.

BEST OLD CITY NARGILEH CAFES
> Derviş Aile Çay Bahçesi (p49)
> Erenler Aile Çay Bahçesi (p68)
> Lale Bahçesi (p69)
> Yeni Marmara (p49)

BEST BEYOĞLU NARGILEH CAFES
> Perla Kallâvi Nargileh Cafe (p93)
> Tophane Nargileh Cafes (p93)

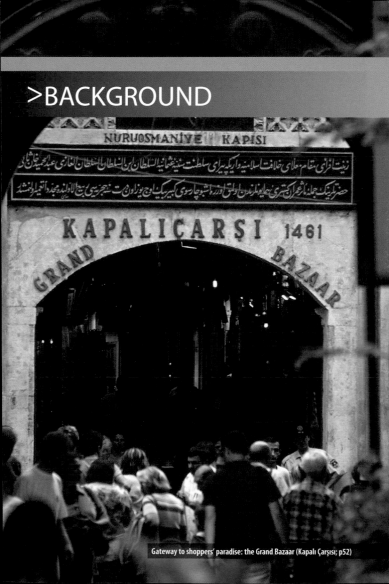

>BACKGROUND

NURUOSMANIYE KAPISI

KAPALIÇARSI 1461

GRAND BAZAAR

Gateway to shoppers' paradise: the Grand Bazaar (Kapalı Çarşısı; p52)

BACKGROUND
HISTORY
If you like your history on an epic scale, you've come to the right place.

BYZANTIUM
In 657 BC, so the story goes, a Greek named Byzas sailed up the Bosphorus in search of a suitable place for a new colony. Before leaving his homeland, he'd asked the Delphic oracle where he should found his settlement. The enigmatic answer he received was 'Opposite the blind'. In one stretch on the eastern shore of the strait Byzas noticed a small colony. Looking to the west, he saw a superb natural harbour and an inviting waterway (which came to be known as the Golden Horn, or Haliç). Thinking that 'Those people on the east side must be blind!', Byzas realised he'd found the site the oracle had prophesied. The colony he founded came to be called Byzantium.

Byzantium survived for centuries by submitting to imperial powers. It finally made the mistake of supporting the wrong side in a Roman civil war; the winner, Septimius Severus, razed the city walls in AD 196. When he rebuilt the city, he renamed it Augusta Antonina.

CONSTANTINOPLE
In 324, Emperor Constantine, vying for control of the Roman Empire, pursued his rival Licinius to Augusta Antonina. After defeating Licinius, Constantine laid out a vast new city to serve as his capital; this 'New Rome' was named Constantinople and inaugurated with much pomp in 330.

Constantine died in 337, just seven years after the dedication of Constantinople, but the city continued to grow under the rule of the succeeding emperors. Theodosius I (the Great) had a forum built on the present site of Beyazıt Square, while his son Theodosius II built the Theodosian Walls in 413 when the city was threatened by the armies of Attila the Hun. The walls he built still surround the Old City today.

Theodosius II died in 450 and and was succeeded by a string of rulers, including the man who would become known as the most famous of all of the Byzantine emperors, Justinian (r 527–65). With his wife Theodora (see p142), Justinian further embellished Constantinople with great buildings, including the famous Aya Sofya (537). However, Justinian's ambitious building projects and constant wars of reconquest exhausted his treasure and his empire. Following his reign, the Byzantine Empire would never again be as large, powerful or rich.

THE CONQUEST

The Ottoman sultan Mehmet II, known to history as Fatih (the Conqueror), inherited the throne of Osman in 1451 and immediately decided to conquer the once great Byzantine city.

In four short months, Mehmet oversaw the building of Rumeli Hisarı (Fortress of Europe), the great fortress on the European side of the Bosphorus, as well as the repair of Anadolu Hisarı (Fortress of Anatolia), built half a century earlier by his great-grandfather Beyazıt I. Together these fortresses controlled the strait's narrowest point.

The Byzantines had closed the mouth of the Golden Horn with a heavy chain (parts of which are on view in the İstanbul Archaeology Museums, p38) to prevent Ottoman boats from sailing in and attacking the city walls on the northern side. Not to be thwarted, Mehmet marshalled his ships at the cove where the Dolmabahçe Palace now stands, and used rollers to transport them up the valley and down the other side into the Golden Horn at Kasımpaşa. Catching the Byzantine defenders by surprise, he soon had the Golden Horn under control.

The last great obstacle was provided by the city's mighty walls on the western side. No matter how heavily Mehmet's cannons battered them, the Byzantines rebuilt them by night and, come daybreak, the impetuous young sultan would find himself back where he'd started. Finally, he received a proposal from a Hungarian cannon maker called Urban, who had come to help the Byzantine emperor defend Christendom against the infidels. Finding that the Byzantine emperor had no money, Urban instead offered to make Mehmet the largest cannon the world had ever seen. Mehmet gladly accepted, and the mighty cannon breached the walls on 28 May 1453, allowing the Ottomans into the city. By the evening of the 29th they were in complete control. The last Byzantine emperor, Constantine XI Dragases, died fighting on the walls.

THE OTTOMAN CENTURIES

Mehmet began to rebuild and repopulate the city immediately. He chose the promontory Saray Burnu (Seraglio Point) as the site for his palace, Topkapı, and repaired and fortified the Theodosian Walls. İstanbul was soon the administrative, commercial and cultural heart of his growing empire.

POWERS BEHIND THE THRONE

Many powerful women have featured in İstanbul's imperial history. These are our favourites:

Theodora

In his *Secret History,* the Roman scholar Procopius wrote that Theodora, the wife of Emperor Justinian, was the daughter of a bear keeper at the Hippodrome. Other accounts assert that she was the daughter of a Roman senator. Whatever her antecedents, Justinian was devoted to his wife, and she was widely acknowledged by contemporary historians to be the power behind the throne. When the Nika riots broke out in 532, the Imperial Council advised the emperor to flee the city, but Theodora persuaded him to stay and fight. The riot was put down and Justinian went on to enjoy a 38-year reign with Theodora at his side.

Zoe

Our favourite of all the empresses, feisty Zoe was 50 years old and supposedly a virgin when her dying father, Constantine VIII, insisted she marry the aged Romanus III Argyrus. When Constantine died, Romanus was crowned emperor and Zoe empress. Finding married life a tad dull, Zoe took as her lover the much younger Michael the Paphlagonian. After Romanus mysteriously drowned in his bath in 1034, Zoe quickly married her virile companion, who joined her on the throne as Michael IV. Eight years later, after Michael died from an illness contracted while on campaign, Zoe and her sister Theodora ruled for a short period as empresses in their own right. Then, at the age of 64, Zoe was married again – to an eminent senator, Constantine IX Monomachus, who eventually outlived her and reigned as Constantine IX until 1055.

Roxelana

The wife of Süleyman the Magnificent, Hürrem Sultan was more commonly known as Roxelana (the Russian). Although Islamic law allowed Süleyman four legal wives and as many concubines as he could support, after meeting Roxelana he was devoted to her alone. Secure in her position, she mastered the art of behind-the-scenes manipulation, even convincing the sultan to have his favourite son by another woman strangled so that her own son Selim (known to history as 'The Sot') could inherit the throne.

The building boom Mehmet kicked off was continued by his successors. The most prodigious builder was Süleyman the Magnificent; aided by Islam's greatest architect, Mimar Koca Sinan (p39), he was responsible for more construction than any other sultan. His endowments to the city include Süleymaniye Mosque (1550), the city's largest mosque.

As the Ottoman Empire grew to encompass the Middle East, North Africa and half of Eastern Europe, İstanbul became a fabulous melting pot of nationalities; it was said that 70 languages could be heard on its streets.

However, by the 19th century Turkey had come to be known as the 'sick man of Europe'. Despite retaining enough allure to attract the first great international luxury express train (the famous *Orient Express*), it was well and truly on the wane.

TURKISH REPUBLIC

In WWI, Turkey sided with old friend Germany, and upon losing was very nearly carved up by the victorious Allies – saved only by the resistance effort led by Mustafa Kemal Pasha (Atatürk), the hero of Çanakkale. Seeking a safe base from which to conduct the nation's liberation struggle, he turned his back on İstanbul and based himself and his colleagues in Ankara, a place free of both imperial associations and the threat of attack by gunboat. When the republic was declared, Ankara was made its capital.

Robbed of its status as capital, İstanbul lost much of its wealth and glitter. Happily, in the last two decades İstanbul has undergone a renaissance. Turkey's bid to join the EU is underpinned by the fact that İstanbul is once again one of the world's most cosmopolitan and sophisticated cities.

LIFE AS AN İSTANBULLU

Walking the streets of İstanbul, you could be forgiven for believing all İstanbullus do is eat out. Indeed, the number of tea gardens, cafes and bars is testimony to the city's vibrant social scene and the fact that good food and good company are the essence of İstanbullu life.

Turks are extremely social people. Family is all-important, as are friends. Everyone feels a sense of responsibility to their neighbours and to children, regardless of whose they are. A stroll to the corner store for a loaf of bread inevitably means a volley of greetings and a chat to neighbours along the way, as well as a short joust with the local kids playing football on the street.

While almost everyone in İstanbul is Muslim, few are devoutly so. Most only attend mosque on the Friday lunchtime prayer session and on any *bayram* (religious holiday). Nevertheless, Islam is a unifying institution, and deeply embedded in the culture.

> **MOSQUE ETIQUETTE**
> > Always remove your shoes before entering a mosque.
> > Wear modest clothes when visiting mosques. Women should have their head, arms and shoulders covered with a shawl, and should wear modest trousers, dresses or skirts, preferably reaching at least to the knees.
> > Avoid entering mosques at prayer time.

The other thing that unites – or, rather, divides – İstanbullus is football. You had better hope you don't find yourself caught between opposing Fenerbahçe and Galatasaray fans, or you can forget everything we said about Turks being sociable!

GOVERNMENT & POLITICS

Though the Turks are firm believers in democracy, the tradition of popular rule is relatively short. Real multiparty democracy came into being only after WWII, and has been interrupted several times by military coups, though government has always eventually been returned to civilians.

The continuing power of the military is embodied in the staunchly secular National Security Council (NSC), which is made up of high-level government and military leaders and meets monthly to advise the government. Its relationship with the ruling Justice & Development Party (AKP) is uneasy, largely due to the NSC's belief that the AKP has an Islamist agenda. When, in 2008, the AKP passed a law (later struck down by the constitutional court) that allowed women to wear the Islamic headscarf at university, the NSC saw this as proof positive of such an agenda. For secular Turks the headscarf (*türban* or *eşarp*) is a symbol of everything they despise and fear – and a total repudiation of everything that Atatürk and his fellow republicans fought for.

In 2010, a national referendum in Turkey saw a majority of the electorate supporting proposed government-sponsored constitutional amendments including giving civilian courts the right to try military personnel, granting public servants the right to collective bargaining, lifting the ban on general strikes and introducing major changes to Constitutional Court that give parliament and the president a greater say in its composition and take away its power to close down political parties (a situation the AKP faced as a result of the 2008 headscarf kerfuffle).

Supporters of the referendum package argue that its reforms have brought Turkey in line with its European neighbours and strengthened its case for EU membership. Opponents, including the main opposition party, the Republican People's Party (CHP), claim that it has weakened the independence of the judiciary and given too much power to the government – opening the door to an Islamist-sponsored assault on Atatürk's secular republic. One consequence is indisputable: a pious and increasingly prosperous Anatolian middle class has become the nation's new major power bloc, lining up behind the AKP to supplant the Turkish military and its associated secular elites.

The current metropolitan city government is led by Kadir Topbaş, who is a member of the AKP. His administration is perceived to be doing a good job of coping with the demands on city infrastructure that the continuing influx of migrants from the provinces is making. It's also considered by most to be doing an excellent job with the provision of municipal services such as transport (particularly the huge and visionary Marmaray Project) and with cleaning up the city's long-polluted waterways. Accusations of corruption and cronyism are of course made from time to time, but overall, voter approval is quite high.

ENVIRONMENT

Apart from the hypergrowth that has plagued İstanbul over the last few decades, the major environmental issue facing the city is the pollution of the Bosphorus by the 45,000 vessels that travel its length annually, 10% of which are tankers. A new oil pipeline running between Azerbaijan and the Turkish eastern Mediterranean port of Ceyhan will alleviate the need for some of this traffic, but until this eventuates a massive amount of toxic substances and oil continues to be carried along the Bosphorus.

İstanbul lies over the North Anatolian Fault, which runs for about 1500km between the Anatolian and Eurasian tectonic plates. Thirteen major earthquakes in Turkey have been recorded since 1939, with the most recent being in 1999. Experts predict that when the next major quake hits the city, much of İstanbul's poorly built outer-suburban development is unlikely to survive.

ORHAN PAMUK

In 2006 Turkey's major literary figure added the Nobel Prize for Literature to his impressive array of prizes and accolades. The only prize Orhan Pamuk hasn't accepted is the prestigious title of state artist, which was offered to him in 1999 by the Turkish government. He refused the title as, he stated, a protest against the government's incarceration of writers, 'narrow-minded nationalism' and its inability to address the Kurdish problem with anything but force. More recently he was charged under the infamous Article 301, which prohibits people from 'insulting Turkishness', after a Swiss magazine quoted him as saying that 30,000 Kurds and one million Armenians had been murdered in Turkey. Charges were dropped in early 2006.

Most critics describe Pamuk's novels as postmodernist, citing similarities to the work of Umberto Eco and Italo Calvino. The most accessible of his books – and a cracking read – is *Snow*, set in the remote eastern town of Kars. *The Black Book*, set in Beyoğlu, was made into a film *(Gizli Yüz)* by Omer Kavur in 1992. *Istanbul: Memories of a City* (aka *Istanbul: Memories and the City*) is a fascinating and highly personal exploration of the author's complex relationship with his beguiling home. Pamuk's most recent novel is *The Museum of Innocence*.

FURTHER READING

While Orhan Pamuk (above) is the most widely translated and best-known Turkish novelist, French-Turkish writer Elif Şafak is also gaining an international reputation. Two of her novels, *The Flea Palace* and *The Bastard of Istanbul,* are set in İstanbul and provide interesting portraits of contemporary İstanbullu society. Like Pamuk, Şafak has been charged with 'insulting Turkishness' under Article 301 – her mistake was to raise the vexed Armenian genocide question in *The Bastard of Istanbul*. The case against her was eventually dismissed due to lack of evidence.

İrfan Orga's autobiographical *Portrait of a Turkish Family,* set during the late Ottoman and early Republican eras, describes the collapse of his well-to-do İstanbullu family and its struggle to rebuild itself, a story that beautifully mirrors the experience of İstanbul itself. Orga's son Ateş is the editor of *Istanbul,* a volume of poetry written about the city. It's part of Eland Books' excellent Poetry of Place series.

Edmondo de Amicis' *Constantinople,* first published in 1877, has been recently translated into English. His evocation of 19th-century İstanbul is masterful and makes for a great read.

Before he became Mr Vita Sackville-West, Harold Nicholson was a diplomat in İstanbul. His extremely moving love story-cum-political thriller, *Sweet Waters,* written in 1921, is set here.

John Freely is *the* authority on İstanbul. His numerous titles, including *Strolling Through Istanbul* (written with Hilary Sumner-Boyd), *Inside the Seraglio* and *Istanbul: The Imperial City,* are all well worth reading for anyone with an interest in the city – we couldn't have written this book without them. His daughter Maureen Freely is Pamuk's English translator and a novelist in her own right; her novel *Enlightenment* is set in İstanbul and addresses weighty issues such as political repression and cultural dislocation.

Mary Wortley Montagu's *Turkish Embassy Letters* details the author's travels to İstanbul in 1716 with her husband, the British ambassador to Turkey. It's a surprisingly nonjudgmental account of life in the heart of the Ottoman Empire.

Describing İstanbul's neighbourhoods with extraordinary colour and detail, Barbara Nadel writes gripping whodunits featuring the chain-smoking, family-loving Inspector Çetin İkmen. Her most recent titles are *Death by Design* (2010) and *A Noble Killing* (2011). See also p108.

Two crime-fiction writers who use Ottoman-era İstanbul as a setting are Jason Goodwin *(The Janissary Tree, The Snake Stone* and *The Bellini Card)* and Jenny White *(The Sultan's Seal* and *The Abyssinian Proof)*, both of which are worth checking out.

FOR THE CD COLLECTION

> *Su* – Mercan Dede is a growing name in hip circles in İstanbul and abroad. *Su* (2003) is best described as Sufi-electronic-techno fusion, and is arguably his best work to date. His albums *Sayahatname* (2001), *Nar* (2002), *Sufi Traveller* (2004) and *Nefes* (2007) are also well worth a listen.

> *Keçe Kurdan* – Aynur's impassioned 2004 folk album, sung entirely in Kurdish, was her excellent debut onto the international scene. It also got her into hot water, a court in Diyarbakır banning it because it 'incites women to take to the hills and promotes division'.

> *Rapstar* – The energy and passion in Ceza's (pronounced *Je-zah*) 2004 rap album is palpable. His most recent album is *Onuncu Köy* (2010).

> *Duble Oryantal* – The now disbanded Baba Zulu were famous for their 'Oriental Dub' and this 2005 fusion album was mixed by the British dub master Mad Professor. Their last album was 2007's *Kökler*.

> *Gipsy Rum* – This 1998 production by Burhan Öçal and the İstanbul Oriental Ensemble is an excellent, thigh-slapping introduction to Turkey's Romany music. *Sultan's Secret Door* (1998) and *Caravansarai* (2001) are also worth a listen.

FILMS

Contemporary directors of note include Ferzan Özpetek, whose 1996 film *Hamam,* set in İstanbul, was a big hit on the international festival circuit and is particularly noteworthy for addressing the hitherto hidden issue of homosexuality in Turkish society.

Nuri Bilge Ceylan's 2003 film *Distant* received a rapturous response from critics and audiences alike when it was released, winning the Jury Prize at the Cannes Film Festival among other accolades. Ceylan's other notable work, *Three Monkeys,* won the Best Director Award at Cannes in 2008.

Turkish-German director Fatih Akın received rave reviews and a screen-writing prize at Cannes for his 2007 film *The Edge of Heaven,* parts of which are set in İstanbul. His film *Head On* won the Golden Bear in Berlin in 2004. The 2005 documentary *Crossing the Bridge: The Sound of İstanbul* is his entertaining snapshot of the local music scene.

Yavuz Turgul's wildly popular 2005 film *Heartache* is the story of ideal-ist Nazim, who returns home to İstanbul after teaching for 15 years in a remote village in eastern Turkey and starts a doomed relationship with a single mother who works in a sleazy bar. It's particularly notable for the soundtrack by Tamer Çıray, which features the voice of Aynur Doğan.

Semih Kaplanoğlu's moving film *Honey* was awarded the Golden Bear Award at the 2010 Berlin Film Festival, and Seren Yüce's *The Majority* was awarded the prize for Best First Feature at the 2010 Venice Film Festival. Yüce worked with Fatih Akın on *The Edge of Heaven.*

Finally, James Bond, the sultan of all secret agents, pops up twice in İstanbul, first in 1963's *From Russia with Love,* and then in 1999's *The World Is Not Enough*. The city provides a great backdrop for his suave manoeuvres and sophisticated seductions.

DIRECTORY
TRANSPORT
ARRIVAL & DEPARTURE
AIR

İstanbul has two international airports, Atatürk International Airport and Sabiha Gökçen International Airport.

Atatürk International Airport

İstanbul's busiest international airport is the **Atatürk International Airport** (Atatürk Havalimanı; code IST; ☎ 212-465 5555; www.ataturkairport.com), 23km west of Sultanahmet.

A taxi between the airport and Sultanahmet or Taksim Square costs around TL35, more if there's heavy traffic.

If you're staying near Taksim Square, the **Havaş airport bus** (☎ 212-244 0487; www.havas.com.tr; 1 way TL10) is the easiest way to get into town. Buses depart from the airport and the square every 15 to 30 minutes from 4am until 1am.

Airport Shuttle (www.istanbulairportshuttle.com; €10pp) operates eight shuttles per day between Atatürk International Airport and Sultanahmet or Taksim. Book in advance and note that if you're taking the shuttle from the city to the airport you should allow lots of time for the trip, as the minibus may spend up to an hour collecting all its passengers before heading out to the airport.

Getting from the airport to Sultanahmet by public transport is cheap and easy. Take the Light Rail Transit (LRT) service from the airport six stops to Zeytinburnu (TL1.50), from where you connect with a tram (TL1.50) that takes you directly to Sultanahmet. If you're staying in Beyoğlu, you should continue on to Kabataş, where the tram connects to the funicular (TL1.50) running up to Taksim Square; the whole trip takes about 50 minutes to S

CLIMATE CHANGE & TRAVEL

Every form of transport that relies on carbon-based fuel generates CO2, the main cause of human-induced climate change. Modern travel is dependent on aeroplanes, which might use less fuel per kilometre per person than most cars but travel much greater distances. The altitude at which aircraft emit gases (including CO2) and particles also contributes to their climate change impact. Many websites offer 'carbon calculators' that allow people to estimate the carbon emissions generated by their journey and, for those who wish to do so, to offset the impact of the greenhouse gases emitted with contributions to portfolios of climate-friendly initiatives throughout the world. Lonely Planet offsets the carbon footprint of all staff and author travel.

ultanahmet, and an extra 20 minutes to Taksim. Services depart every 10 minutes or so from 5.40am until 1.40am.

Sabiha Gökçen International Airport

A smaller airport, **Sabiha Gökçen International Airport** (Sabiha Gökçen Uluslararası Havaalanı; code SAW; ☎ 216-585 5000; www.sgairport.com) is located some 50km east of Sultanahmet and Taksim on the Asian side of the city. It's a lot less convenient to get to than Atatürk International Airport and transport options are limited.

A taxi will take you from the airport to Sultanahmet costs at least TL90; to Taksim it will be at least TL80.

The **Havaş Airport Bus** (☎ 212-444 0487; www.havas.com.tr; TL13) travels between the airport and Taksim. These depart the airport every 30 minutes between 4am and midnight and thereafter when flights land. The trip takes one hour.

Airport Shuttle (www.istanbulairpot shuttle.com; €10pp) runs seven shuttles per day between the airport and Sultanahmet or Taksim – book ahead. Be warned that these services can be slow.

İETT bus E3 travels from the airport to the Levent 4 metro station (TL1.50), where you can connect with the metro to Taksim Square (TL1.50), and then the funicular

(TL1.50) and tram (TL1.50) to Sultanahmet. Be warned, though, that this trip will take hours. The buses operate between 7am and 10.40pm.

Equally complicated and time-consuming is the trip on İETT bus E10 from the airport to Kadıköy (TL1.50), from where you can catch a ferry to Eminönü (TL1.50) and then a tram (TL1.50) up to Sultanahmet. The buses operate between 6.20am to 10.30pm.

TRAIN

All trains from Europe currently terminate at **Sirkeci Train Station** (Map p35, B2; ☎ 212-527 0051; Ankara Caddesi, Sirkeci). Outside the station's main door there's a convenient tram that runs up the hill to Sultanahmet or over the Golden Horn (Haliç) to Kabataş, from where you can travel by funicular up to Taksim Square.

Trains from the Asian side of Turkey and from countries to the east and south currently terminate at **Haydarpaşa Railway Station** (☎ 216-336 4470; Haydarpaşa İstasyon Caddesi, Kadıköy), on the Asian shore close to Kadıköy. Ferries between Eminönü and Kadıköy are cheap and speedy.

VISA

Nationals of the following countries (among others) do not need a visa to visit Turkey for up to

ARRIVING IN İSTANBUL BY TRAIN

The *Orient Express*, running between Paris and Constantinople, is remembered as one of the world's most famous rail journeys. And although it's no longer possible to take this iconic journey to İstanbul, it's still possible to arrive in the city by train.

At the time of writing the only direct train between Western Europe and Turkey was the *Dostluk-Filia Express*, a deluxe overnight train with sleeper cars running between İstanbul and Thessaloniki (Salonica) in Greece, and connecting there with services to Athens.

From eastern Europe, you can travel to İstanbul via the cities of Bucharest, Belgrade and Sofia on the daily *Bosphor/Balkan Express*.

Coming from the Middle East, the *Trans-Aysa Express* travels from Tehran to İstanbul via Van, Kayseri and Ankara once per week.

You can check timetables and book seats through Turkish State Railways (www.tcdd.gov .tr). Also check out Mark Smith's Man in Seat 61 (www.seat61.com), an inspirational resource for rail-travel enthusiasts.

three months: Denmark, Finland, France, Germany, Greece, Italy, Japan, New Zealand, Sweden and Switzerland. Nationals of Australia, Belgium, Canada, Ireland, the Netherlands, Norway, Portugal, Spain, the UK and the USA do need a visa, but this is just a sticker bought on arrival at the airport or border post rather than at an embassy in advance (make sure you join the queue to buy your visa before you queue for immigration). How much you need to pay for your visa varies. At the time of writing, Dutch, Britons, Australians and Americans paid €15 and Canadians paid €45. No photos are required. See the website of the **Ministry of Foreign Affairs** (www.mfa.gov.tr) for the latest information.

GETTING AROUND

Moving some 16 million people around İstanbul is a challenge (understatement of the year), but in the last few years the government has begun to implement the ambitious Marmaray transport project (www.marmaray.com), which aims to ease the city's horrendous traffic problems. Thankfully most of the major sights you'll want to see on a short visit to the city are within walking distance or a short tram or bus ride away. In this book, each listing notes transport options from Sultanahmet.

TRAVEL PASSES

If you're in town for a week or so, it makes sense to purchase one of the electronic public transport cards that were introduced in 2009. These can be used on the city's ferries, İETT buses, LRT, trams, metro and funiculars.

The İstanbulkart is similar to London's Oyster Card, Hong Kong's Octopus Card and Paris' Navigo, offering convenience and a slight discount on fares. The card costs TL10 and can be charged with amounts in multiples of TL5. They're simple to operate: as you enter a bus or pass through the turnstile at a ferry dock or metro station, swipe your card for entry and the fare will automatically be deducted from your balance.

The non-rechargeable beşiBiryerde Card is named after traditional Turkish jewellery consisting of five pieces of gold. The five-fare card costs TL7.50.

Note that at the time of research, both cards were proving hard to access. Ideally, they should be available for purchase and recharging at machines at ferry docks, metro stations and bus stations. Ask your hotel for an update on their status, price and availability.

TRAM

An excellent *tramvay* (tramway) service runs from Zeytinburnu

Transport Times Between Key Destinations

	Aya Sofya	Grand Bazaar	Eminönü	Chora Church	Galata Tower	Taksim Square
Aya Sofya	n/a	walk 10min	walk 15min; tram 7min	car 20min	walk 45min; tram 15min	tram 20min then funicular 2min
Grand Bazaar	walk 10min	n/a	walk 15min	car 15min	walk 30min	tram 30min then funicular 2min
Eminönü	walk 15min; tram 7min	walk 15min	n/a	car 15min	walk 15min	tram 10min then funicular 2min
Chora Church	car 20min	car 15min	car 15min	n/a	car 15min	car 20min
Galata Tower	walk 45min; tram 15min	walk 30min	walk 15min	car 15min	n/a	walk 25min
Taksim Square	tram 20min then funicular 2min	tram 30min then funicular 2min	tram 10min then funicular 2min	car 20min	walk 25min	n/a

(where it connects with the airport LRT) to Sultanahmet and Eminönü, and then across the Galata Bridge (Galata Köprüsü) to Karaköy (to connect with the funicular to Tünel Square) and Kabataş (to connect with the funicular to Taksim Square). Trams run every five minutes or so from 6am to midnight. Tickets cost TL1.50.

FUNICULAR RAILWAY
A *funiküler* (funicular) known as the Tünel runs from Karaköy to Tünel Square at the end of İstiklal Caddesi (TL1).

Another funicular runs from Kabataş, at the end of the tramline, up the hill to the metro station at Taksim Square (TL1.50).

Services are frequent on both lines, trips take approximately three minutes.

BUS
İstanbul Elektrik Tramvay ve Tünel (İETT) buses are run by the city and you must have a ticket (TL1.50 per trip) on many, but not all, services before boarding. You can buy tickets from the white booths near major stops or from some nearby shops for a small mark-up (look for *İETT otobüs bileti satılır* signs). Think about buying a travelcard (p151) to avoid this.

BOAT
The most enjoyable and efficient way to get around town is by ferry. **İstanbul Deniz Otobüsleri** (☎ 212-444 4436; www.ido.com.tr) has timetable information, or you can pick up a printed timetable at a ferry dock. A *jeton* (transport token) costs TL1.50 for most routes (not the Bosphorus Excursion Ferry); it's possible to use travelcards (p151) on all routes.

The main ferry docks are at the mouth of the Golden Horn (Eminönü, Sirkeci and Karaköy), Beşiktaş, Üsküdar, Kadıköy and Kabataş, just south of Dolmabahçe Palace.

TAXI
İstanbul is full of yellow taxis. Flagfall is TL2.50 and the rate per km is TL1.50. There are no evening surcharges.

Taxi rates are very reasonable – from Sultanahmet to Taksim Square will cost around TL12; ignore taxi drivers who insist on a fixed rate as these are much higher than you'd pay using the meter. Double-check the money you give the driver too: drivers have been known to insist they were given a TL5 note for payment, when they were really given TL20.

LIGHT RAIL TRANSIT (LRT)
An efficient LRT service connects Aksaray with Atatürk International Airport, stopping at 15 stations, including the International İstanbul Bus Station, known simply as the *otogar* (bus station), along the way. Services depart every 10 minutes or so from 5.40am until 1.40am. Tickets cost TL1.50.

METRO
A modern metro system connects Şişhane, near Tünel Square in Beyoğlu, with Atatürk Oto Sanayi in Maslak, the city's financial centre. Unfortunately, it's not possible to travel between the two points in one trip – one metro runs between Şişhane and Taksim Square; another runs between Taksim and Levent 4; and a third runs between Levent 4 and Atatürk Oto Sanayi. The full trip takes 30 to 40 minutes. Services run every five minutes or so from approximately 6.30am to midnight. Tickets cost TL1.50.

PRACTICALITIES
BUSINESS HOURS
Government departments, offices and banks usually open from 8.30am to noon and 1.30pm to 5pm Monday to Friday. Shops are generally open from 9am to 6pm Monday to Saturday, but shops in the Sultanahmet area will open until 10pm or later if it's very busy, and will also open on Sunday. Most museums close on Monday.

EMERGENCIES
Although İstanbul is by no means a dangerous city, it's wise to be a little cautious. Be wary of pickpockets in buses and crowded places, particularly the Grand Bazaar (Kapalı Çarşı), Eminönü, Galata Bridge (Galata Köprüsü) and İstiklal Caddesi.

Pedestrians should give way to cars in all situations, even if you have to jump out of the way.

In İstanbul single men are sometimes lured to bars by new Turkish 'friends', and then are forced (sometimes with violence) to pay an outrageous bill. Drugging is also a serious risk, so be a tad wary about who you befriend.

See the inside front cover for emergency phone numbers.

HOLIDAYS
There are five secular public holidays per year.
New Year's Day 1 January
National Sovereignty & Children's Day 23 April
Youth & Sports Day 19 May
Victory Day 30 August
Republic Day 29 October
Religious festivals are celebrated according to the Muslim lunar

MAJOR ISLAMIC HOLIDAYS

Dates in this table are estimates; exact dates are not confirmed until the moon is sighted.

Ramazan begins	Şeker Bayramı	Kurban Bayramı
1 Aug 2011	30 Aug 2011	5 Nov 2011
20 Jul 2012	19 Aug 2012	24 Oct 2012

Hejira calendar; two of these festivals (Şeker Bayramı and Kurban Bayramı) are also public holidays. Şeker Bayramı is a three-day festival at the end of Ramazan, and Kurban Bayramı, the most important religious holiday of the year, is a four-day festival. During these festivals, banks and offices are closed, and hotels, buses, trains and planes are heavily booked.

During the Holy Month of Ramazan, called Ramadan in other Muslim countries, most restaurants and cafes open to serve non-Muslims. It's polite to avoid ostentatious public smoking, eating, drinking and drunkenness during Ramazan.

INTERNET

Ministry of Culture and Tourism (www.turizm.gov.tr) Government information on tourism, culture, archaeology and history.
My Merhaba (www.mymerhaba.com) Expats' website with comprehensive background briefing on the city and Turkish culture.

TimeOut İstanbul (www.timeoutistanbul.com) Official site of the monthly magazine; it's good for drinking, clubbing and eating listings.
Today's Zaman (www.todayszaman.com) Website of the English-language daily newspaper.
Turkey Travel Planner (www.turkeytravelplanner.com) An ever-growing site put together by well-known writer and Turkey expert Tom Brosnahan.

LANGUAGE

Once you learn a few basic rules, Turkish pronunciation is quite simple to master.

İ i	a short 'i', as in 'hit' or 'sit'
I ı	a neutral vowel; as the 'a' in 'ago'
Ö ö	as the 'e' in 'her' said with pursed lips (but with no 'r' sound)
U u	as in 'pull'
Ü ü	an exaggerated rounded-lip 'you'
C c	as the 'j' in 'jet'
Ç ç	as the 'ch' in 'church'
G g	always hard as in 'garden'
Ğ ğ	silent; lengthens preceding vowel
J j	as the 'z' in 'azure'
Ş ş	as the 'sh' in 'show'

ESSENTIALS

Hello.	*Merhaba.*
How are you?	*Nasılsınız?*
I'm fine.	*İyiyim.*
Goodbye.	*Hoşçakal.*
Excuse me.	*Bakar mısınız.*
Yes/No.	*Evet/Hayır.*

Please.	Lütfen.
Thank you.	Teşekkür ederim.
You're welcome.	Birşey değil.
Do you speak English?	İngilizce konuşuyor musunuz?
I don't understand.	Anlamıyorum.
How much is it?	Ne kadar?
That's too expensive.	Bu çok pahalı.
Today.	Bugün.
Tomorrow.	Yarın.
Yesterday.	Dün.

NUMBERS

0	sıfır
1	bir
2	iki
3	üç
4	dört
5	beş
6	altı
7	yedi
8	sekiz
9	dokuz
10	on
11	on bir
12	on iki
21	yirmi bir
100	yüz
1000	bin

EMERGENCIES

I'm sick.	Hastayım.
Help!	İmdat!
Call the police.	Polis çağırın.
Call an ambulance.	Ambulans çağırın.

EATING & DRINKING

(That was) Delicious!	Nefisti!
I'm a vegetarian	Ben vejeteryanım.
Please bring the bill.	Hesap, lütfen.

Local Specialities

baklava – layered filo pastry with honey and nuts

cacık – yoghurt with grated cucumber and mint

dolma – vine or cabbage leaves stuffed with rice

döner kebap – meat packed onto a vertical skewer, then roasted and sliced off

imam bayıldı – eggplant slow-cooked in oil with tomatoes, onions and garlic

karışık ızgara – mixed grill (lamb)

köfte – meatballs

lokum – Turkish delight

rakı – aniseed brandy

şiş kebap – cubes of meat grilled on a skewer

MONEY

Turkey's currency is the Türk Lirası (Turkish Lira; TL). See the inside front cover for exchange rates or check out www.xe.com.

You can xpect to pay around TL120 to TL250 per person per day while staying in a midrange hotel, sightseeing and eating out in İstanbul.

ORGANISED TOURS

İstanbul Vision City Sightseeing Bus
(☎ 212-234 7777; www.plantours.com;
one-day ticket adult/student & 6-12yr/under
6yr €20/15/free) This is a naff hop-on-hop-off
double-decker bus service with multilanguage
recorded commentary. Ticket booths are
opposite Aya Sofya and in Taksim Square. The
full circuit takes 90 minutes, or you can get on
and off the bus at six stops around town (note
that buses only run four times per day from
November to March and nine times per day
from April to October). Expect traffic conges-
tion on the Beyoğlu section.

İstanbul Walks (☎ 212-292 2874; 5th fl,
İstiklal Caddesi 53, Beyoğlu; www
.istanbulwalks.net; walking tours adult/
student & over 65/children under 12 €20/16/
free) Specialising in cultural tourism, this
small company offers a large range of guided
walking tours conducted by knowledgeable
English-speaking guides. Tours concentrate
on the city's various neighbourhoods, but
there are also tours to major monuments
including Aya Sofya, Topkapı Palace and the
İstanbul Archaeology Museums. Of note are
its excellent tour of the Grand Bazaar (€20)
and the 'Dining Out in a Turkish Way' evening
(€60), in which participants are taken to a
traditional teahouse, an *ocakbaşı* (barbecue
restaurant), an *işkembecisi* (tripe soup shop), a
meyhane (tavern) and a nargileh cafe.

TELEPHONE

Turkey uses the standard GSM
(Global System for Mobile Com-
munications) network operating
on 900MHz or 1800MHz bands;
only some US-, Canadian-, and
Scandinavian-bought mobile

WHAT'S ON?

For an overview of what's on, make
sure you pick up a copy of *TimeOut
İstanbul* (www.timeoutistanbul
.com/toi) as soon as you hit town.
Also check **Biletix** (☎ 216-556 9800;
www.biletix.com). Biletix outlets are
found throughout the city, but the
most convenient for travellers is the
one at the **Beyoğlu İstiklal Kitabevi**
(Map pp72-3, E1; İstiklal Caddesi 55,
Beyoğlu).

phones are not compatible.
Mobiles can connect with Turkey's
Turkcell (www.turkcell.com.tr), **Vodafone**
(www.vodafone.com.tr, in Turkish) or **Avea**
(www.avea.com.tr) networks. See the
inside front cover for telephone
codes and useful numbers.

TIPPING

In the cheapest restaurants, locals
leave a few coins in the change
tray. In other restaurants you
should tip about 10% to 15% of
the bill.

It's usual to round-up metered
taxi fares to the nearest 50 kuruş,
so round up TL4.60 to TL5.

TOURIST INFORMATION

There are tourist information
offices in the international arrivals
hall at **Atatürk International Airport**
(☽ 24hr), at **Sirkeci Railway Station**
(Map p34, A2; ☽ 8.30am-5pm) and in

Sultanahmet (Map p35, B4; ☉ 8.30am-5pm). Over the Golden Horn, there's an office in front of the İstanbul Hilton Hotel in **Elmadağ** (☉ 10am-5pm Mon-Sat), about five minutes' walk north of Taksim Square. Note that the Sirkeci Station office will close when the station undergoes its planned redevelopment as part of the Marmaray project, and the Elmadağ office will relocate to the Atatürk Cultural Centre on Taksim Square when that building's redevelopment is complete.

TRAVELLERS WITH DISABILITIES

The bad news is İstanbul can be challenging for mobility-impaired travellers. Roads are potholed and pavements are often crooked and cracked.

The good news is government-run museums are free of charge for disabled visitors, and many of these have wheelchair access. Also, all public transport is free for the disabled and both the LRT (p154) and *tramvay* (p152) can be accessed by people in wheelchairs.

>INDEX

See also separate subindexes for See (p163), Do (p164), Shop (p164), Eat (p166), Drink (p167) and Play (p167).

◉ SEE

000 map pages

INDEX

🍴 EAT

Anatolian

Asian

Baklava

Börek

Delicatessens

Fish

International

Italian

Kebaps

Köfte

Lokantas

Mediterranean

Meyhanes

Organic

Ottoman & Turkish

000 map pages